I0820256

WHO'S WATCHING SHORTY?

WHO'S WATCHING SHORTY?

RECLAIMING MYSELF FROM THE SHAME OF R. KELLY'S ABUSE

RESHONA LANDFAIR

WITH ERICA SIMONE TURNIPSEED

LEGACY LIT

NEW YORK BOSTON

Legacy Lit
Hachette Book Group
1290 Avenue of the Americas
New York, NY 10104
HachetteBookGroup.com
@LegacyLitBooks

First Edition: February 2026

Legacy Lit is an imprint of Grand Central Publishing. The Legacy Lit name and logo are registered trademarks of Hachette Book Group, Inc.

Print book interior design by Marie Mundaca

Library of Congress Cataloging-in-Publication Data has been applied for.

ISBNs: 978-1-5387-7695-7 (hardcover); 978-1-5387-6790-0 (ebook)

Printed in Canada

MRQ-T

10 9 8 7 6 5 4 3 2 1

For Dad, my son, and my inner self

AUTHOR'S NOTE

IN THIS BOOK MANY of my conversations with Robert Kelly, my parents, and others appear in quotation marks. I am not suggesting in this way that these are literal, verbatim transcripts of conversations that, in some cases, happened as far back as twenty-five years ago. Rather, these are reconstructions to the best of my recollection that I am confident accurately reflect the substance and tenor of what was said and done. The substance of these traumatic events is indelibly etched in my mind.

"For I know the plans I have for you," declares the Lord, "plans to prosper you and not to harm you, plans to give you hope and a future."

—Jeremiah 29:11 (NIV)

These muthafuckas ain't stoppin' me.

—Beyonce, *Renaissance*

CONTENTS

FOREWORD

I'M CALLING ON THE cavalry to read this book. We need you.

Black women and girls have been waiting for someone to stand up and protect us for half of a millennium. Reshona Landfair has been waiting a quarter of a century to be seen. In this brave and beautiful memoir, Reshona emerges as a dynamic and resilient adult to tell her story in her own words for the first time.

She owes us nothing, but she has given us a gift.

Reshona Landfair's name was not immediately familiar to me. Although I vividly recalled the rampant innuendo unleashed sometime in 2002 by a widely circulated child sex abuse tape involving music superstar R. Kelly, I remembered nothing about the girl at its center. The details may elude me because I was grappling with my own escape from abuse in the music industry that same year. As a survivor of sexual violence, I made a point of avoiding any footage of the ubiquitous video. In spite of my best efforts, the incessant buzz about the material made it impossible for me to remain totally ignorant of its contents.

Looking back now, I remember hearing about a fast girl, a porn star, or a sex slave who had been defiled, in a number of ways, by a man in his thirties. Not once did I hear this gravely imperiled teenager referred to as someone's daughter or as a child of God. No one expressed any interest in how she got there, or where she came from, or what happened to her after the camera stopped rolling.

Why didn't anyone care?

The answer to that question is arguably white supremacy's crowning achievement. Reshona's abuse, and our callous indifference to it, are heartbreaking installments in the long history of sexual exploitation inflicted on Black women and girls in America. Our casual acceptance of her undeniable suffering reflects centuries of grooming. After all, the institution of slavery was America's economic foundation and depended on the unmitigated rape of Black women and girls. In a society where Black people had no legal rights, there was no room for us to be horrified by their treatment. No opportunity to intervene. For 246 years, our collective psyche found a way to endure unrelenting brutality. So by the time the grown folks who should have rescued Reshona from R. Kelly saw her on that tape, they had been conditioned, along with all of us, not to give a damn.

I know something about this.

In late 2017, during the initial wave of the #MeToo movement, I shared my experiences as a victim of sexual abuse in the music industry in an article in *The New York Times*. Three years later I appeared in a documentary called *On the Record* exploring the double-bind faced by Black female victims of Black perpetrators, as most violent crime, including rape, is intraracial.

It was terrifying.

The challenge of coming forward is exacerbated for Black women by the legacy of false allegations of sexual misconduct that have been weaponized against Black men and boys for centuries. Informed by this history, I intended to carry the secret of my abuse to my grave.

Cases like Emmitt Till and the Exonerated Five weighed heavily on my mind. I was also deterred from coming forward by the contempt with which Anita Hill's story of abuse had been received the year before I began my career in the music industry.

Even without the additional layer of prejudices, reporting sexual abuse is daunting for survivors of all races and genders. The most obvious obstacle is the tremendous shame associated with the experience itself. Coming forward is further complicated by the fact that rape almost always takes place in the context of longstanding interpersonal relationships.

In 2017, struck by the courage of women—and some men—who were bravely calling out abuse by titans in various industries, I decided to break my silence. As a wife, at that time, and as a mother, I felt a responsibility to try to make the world safer for the next generation. As a Black survivor, it was also important to me that the #MeToo movement included our voices. I naively believed that in response to our stories, a phalanx of esteemed leaders would step forward to insist that Black women deserved dignity, safety, and care. I was wrong.

The cavalry for Black women never came.

Black women, expected to be magic, are deprived of the compassion reserved for damsels in distress, so there is no manager or knight in shining armor we can call. Spurned by leaders in our own community, the survivors in *On the Record* joined Reshona Landfair and Anita Hill on a bleak arc of history bending toward despair.

But joy cometh in the morning.

Reshona Landfair grew up. Reshona Landfair set herself free. Reshona Landfair has returned to tell her story. Her unflinchingly honest and deftly told account offers all of us an opportunity to take accountability for our role in her suffering. Hold space for her. Do not look away. We should be horrified. It is not too late for us to intervene, and we must intervene, for the sake of every victim, past and present. They still need you. Reshona still needs you. Black women and girls still need you, and I implore you to give a damn.

Drew Dixon
October 5, 2025

WHO'S WATCHING SHORTY?

PREFACE

FOOLISH GIRL

WHAT WAS THAT FOOLISH girl thinking?

If my brain had not been such a tidal wave of conflicted emotions, shame, and a hazy understanding of love for the grown man who defiled my child's body, maybe I would have asked the same thing. God knows, I often felt foolish, reckless, and ashamed. But most days, I was so paralyzed with fear that I couldn't allow myself to think an answer that Robert hadn't told me to think. This man more than twice my age, whom I called my godfather, made me as invested in his lies as he was.

Was it foolish to believe him when he said that the world hated me, that you thought I was a ho on my best day, but that *he* would protect me? I already knew that nobody could see what was happening. Or if you did, you surely didn't see it as a problem or blame Robert.

I tell you, it's not easy being a girl, especially a Black girl. Shamed for our developing bodies, we're considered too foolish or too fast to keep ourselves outside the clutches of lecherous men. Men who our community puts on a pedestal despite their predatory behavior because of their great music, money, fame, looks, or street cred. And if shit happens, we girls are supposed to lick our wounds quietly and protect our violators' secrets as our own.

Was I a fool to believe Robert when he said I had *made* him love me so hard it hurt? How did I allow myself to get turned out by my godfather? Why didn't I muster the courage to drop a dime on him? After all, there were always plenty of folks milling around. From Robert's parade of bodyguards, cooks, chauffeurs, housekeepers, nannies, sound engineers, musicians, personal assistants, managers, and throngs of other hangers-on to the revolving door of artists and celebrities who were always stopping by, you all saw me there. I was *always* there.

Maybe you looked without seeing.

Maybe you saw without watching. Because if you were watching, you would have seen me seek his approval for every word that came out of my mouth. You would have noticed that all the things that used to matter to me no longer did.

Maybe recognizing my pain would have forced you to unearth the secret of your own abuse and acknowledge your scars from poorly healed trauma.

Perhaps you told yourself it was none of your business. That R. Kelly was no better or worse than any other man in the music game and I should have known better. That somebody else was supposed to check for Shorty because that was above your pay grade. So, because I didn't starve myself of the heady diet of dopamine and adrenaline fed to me by the predator I thought was my lover, *shrug*.

Everybody was looking, after all. But nobody was watching. Not watching me, not watching the man who would cruise the

Rock'n'Roll McDonald's looking for shapely Black girls who seemed to have a point of vulnerability he could exploit.

When Dave Chappelle's "Piss on You" skit aired in early 2003, it added insult to injury for eighteen-year-old me. Here I was, just a few months out from the trauma of the whole world witnessing the disgusting things Robert Sylvester Kelly (R. Kelly to you) did to me and that he compelled me to vehemently deny, and *now* there was a whole *Chappelle's Show* skit poking fun at my humiliation. I'm sure Chappelle would say that comedians make fun of inappropriate stuff all the time. And all of you who laughed at the punch line would argue you weren't laughing at me. But it didn't matter; the damage was done.

Robert was so mad that his threats to me to keep me denying this ever happened often came in the form of physical and psychological abuse. (Ironically, any blows to the chin that Robert took when the shit hit the fan only got him bigger music sales from an even broader audience.) And my ears were always burning from the crass jokes and clucking tongues of friends, neighbors, and church members talking about the girl who got herself peed on. Every now and then, some folks would feel sorry for "that foolish girl." Some of you even cried foul; this was child pornography and statutory rape. But from where I stood, those voices were quickly drowned out by insults: that I was fast, a thirsty and foolhardy groupie, a gold digger, a Jezebel. And my family was riding the gravy train.

Predators know how to find their prey. Robert hunted girls like me: girls with big dreams and naive minds who would believe the lies of a grown-ass man. As much as it sucks to say it, Robert the predator found the right one in me. From the time I was twelve, he fed me his lies—whether silver-tongued and sweet or soul crushing and damning—until they became my own.

Me: Robert is a devoted godfather teaching me the inner workings of the music business.

Also me: Ours is a real but forbidden love. That's why it hurts and feels scary.

I claim no more ownership of Robert's secrets and lies that contaminated my mind and deceived my heart. That means I've got to set the record straight. I know that those lies have made some folks mistrust me. I get it. I can't force anyone to believe me. But if you've ever known crippling fear and shame, if you've ever been so exploited and manipulated that it seemed like all the exit signs were removed from every door, if you've ever been told you caused your own violation and that you're nasty and beyond repair when you're young and vulnerable, maybe you can relate.

When I first started to write this book, I worried about how everyone whose name would be in it would feel. Would I hurt you? Would you hate me? Then I realized that folks who were inclined to hate me already did. And those of you who branded me a liar are free to believe whatever you want about me. I can't live the rest of my existence trying to make everyone feel better about your role in my life. All I can do is tell the truth—as I knew it then and as I know it now—and let the chips fall where they may.

I have no desire to ruin folks' lives. God knows, I've suffered enough under a man who didn't love me like he said he did and was willing to use me up to distract himself from his own demons. I don't wish that kind of misery on anyone. But my path to healing and wholeness means laying down the burden of other people's dishonesty. I refuse to compromise myself and pollute the truth so folks can save face. Embarrassment sucks, but it isn't the end of the story for any of us.

As a full-grown woman, I've come to know a few things about human nature. I know that lots of times, human beings don't operate with pure intentions. Sure, we want to help someone, but we also want to set the table for our own feast. We're angling for a foot in the door or on the ladder of success. We want bragging rights, access to the VIP room, recognition from friends and fans. And if we can't get those things from our own accomplishments, we'll settle for being close enough to the so-called greatness of others that we can grab some of their crumbs.

Lots of folks wanted to rub shoulders with R. Kelly. His R&B empire was so big that hundreds of people could feast on his crumbs. So people protected Robert from scrutiny: for his illiteracy; his cheating on his then wife, Andrea Kelly; and especially his sexual abuse of me, a whole bunch of women, girls, and the boy he called his little nephew. Robert was powerful enough to green-light or bury folks in the music business. Plenty of people knew he was a snake, but since the business is full of snakes, they just decided to tread lightly.

I'm not here to tell those stories or clear anyone's name. But I will not sidestep the hard truth about those people who lied for me and about me, or who encouraged me to lie to protect myself and others. Robert Sylvester Kelly groomed me to fill my mouth, mind, body, and spirit with the filth he fed me. I own the decisions I made, decisions born of warped understanding, fear, confusion, jealousy, and a misguided belief that on the other side of all the lies there would be peace. I've come to realize that as long as the devil is getting the glory in your story, there will *never* be peace.

As I heal the girl inside of me, I'm telling her story, *my* story. I'm reclaiming my name because I don't want it to be a dirty word and my body because I no longer want my image reduced to the blacked-out face of an exploited child. My story may be rough, but *I'm* not a mistake, nor is my life *just* about suffering and tragedy. That's why I'm raising my voice, stepping out of the shadows, and reintroducing myself. Because I know there's a blessing in it—for me and maybe for you, too.

I'm not holding on to one more lie.

PROLOGUE

WESTSIDE SHORTY

KRIS KROSS. LIL' BOW Wow. Me. I was *that* good. A pint-sized girl rapper from the West Side of Chicago, I was a member of a professional singing group called 4 The Cause (originally YWFC, Young Warriors For The Cause), along with three of my cousins, since I was nine. I was the youngest member by a couple of years, but because I was a confident rapper in a small package, I was a standout in the group. Friends, family, and fans alike called me Shorty.

4 The Cause was a cover band, and we put our own hip-hop spin on soul and pop classics like "Stand by Me," "Every Time You Go Away," and "Ain't No Sunshine," as well as original songs like "Make Your Head Rock." At first, we were on football legend Reggie White's record label, Big Doggie Records, before signing with Jurgen Grebner, who was then at RCA/BMG. (By 1998, we had released a CD and were minor celebrities in Europe and beyond; our song "Stand by Me" even charted in the Top 10 in eight countries: Germany—where it reached number two—as well as Austria,

Belgium, Ireland, the Netherlands, New Zealand, Sweden, and Switzerland.) Although 4 The Cause toured in several countries, especially Germany and Italy, our group's popularity in the U.S. was more modest; most of our stateside fans were in our Chicago hometown. But my family kept me humble, and at nine, ten, eleven, and twelve years old, I really didn't realize that our group was internationally famous. With my dad, Greg Landfair Sr., a professional guitarist, and my favorite aunt, Stephanie "Sparkle" Edwards, an R&B singer on the come-up in Chicago, I was just loving life and following in the footsteps of my musical family.

Music wasn't the only thing I loved to do, though. My tiny frame contained a big and bubbly personality, and I was popular in my Oak Park neighborhood for being a tomgirl who delivered on the basketball court, a Girl Scout who took my cookie sales seriously, and a leader among my peers. My family was nobody's idea of rich, but if there was ever any struggle, it lived far beyond my notice. As far as I was concerned, life was full of everything I needed and a few extras besides. I loved being a big sister to my brother, lil Greg, who's eight years younger than me. As short and small as I was, I was a giant to him; when I picked him up and put him on my shoulders, I relished how good it felt to be big and powerful in his eyes. My parents kept me active in our community, from attending a host of local park and rec center events to being an intercessor and praise dancer at our family's church. Since we lived pretty close to my grandparents, cousins, aunts, and uncles on both sides of my family, they were like a safety net that extended my footprint beyond my neighborhood and tapped me in to everything else that was fun in my corner of the globe in the 1990s.

I wouldn't say I had stars in my eyes, but I lived in a world of big aspirations. As Greg Landfair's daughter, Sparkle's niece, and

Shorty the rapper, I definitely enjoyed opportunities to try on what it was like to be a celebrity artist. If you asked me, I probably would have said I wanted to make it big as a rapper or basketball player. Maybe both! And with my ambitious and tight-knit family, I had no doubt I'd get wherever I wanted to go.

PART ONE

I WANNA BE DOWN

I could be wrong, but I feel like something could be going on.

—Brandy

CHAPTER 1

ALL THAT GLITTERS

I DON'T KNOW HOW it happened, but when I was twelve, I was my aunt Sparkle's mini–best girlfriend. Or at least that's what it seemed like, and I felt special. She was known to the rest of the world as Sparkle, but to me, she was my beautiful, glamorous, and talented aunt. Sparkle—aka my mom's youngest sister, Stephanie—was *already* the celebrity of our family, well before her first album was ever released. At sixteen years my senior (nine if you're counting by her music-industry age), Aunt Sparkle lived downtown, traveled at whim, and had choreographers and producers as friends. She was different. I admired everything about her.

When I was very little, I remember, I met the man who was then Aunt Sparkle's husband: Earl Robinson of the R&B trio Public Announcement. The group became best known on the national scene for backing an up-and-coming R. Kelly in the early 1990s. The day I met him at my grandmother's house, his combat boots, new jack swing outfit, and swagger told me he was big-time even before Aunt Sparkle introduced him. That was how she rolled, too: hair laid, outfit on point, and her own swagger that made people take notice.

At some point, Aunt Sparkle no longer had a husband, but what she told twelve-year-old me confirmed she had her share of admirers and hadn't lost a step in her personal life. As I watched her get dressed to the nines for her various engagements, she would school me on topics that felt light-years away, like the importance of staying ready for a sexual encounter by keeping my vagina on fleek.

I twisted my face into a question mark.

Aunt Sparkle stopped putting on her makeup. Reading my face, she sighed at the question I didn't ask. "Chon, wouldn't it be easier to keep your head clean if you had no hair?"

"I guess." I hunched my shoulders.

"And isn't it easier to see someone's lips if they don't have a beard?"

"Yeah..."

"It's the same with our vaginas, Chon. Even if you don't want to share yours with anyone else just yet, you will one day. Just take my word on *that*. And that's *not* the time to learn how to keep her cute and sweet." She wrinkled her face. "Best to stay ready so you don't have to get ready!" Aunt Sparkle tapped my nose with her manicured finger like she had made everything clear.

Even as I puzzled over her advice, I was sure of one thing: My aunt was the big sister I never had, and her sensational life felt like a peek behind the veil of womanhood.

She didn't say that our conversations were a secret, but I knew they weren't for public consumption either, so I kept her revelations to myself...mostly. Hearing her stories of sexual encounters with high-profile men and her various boyfriends in the music industry filled my imagination with PG-13 daydreams, but I didn't want to discourage her from sharing them. Aunt Sparkle knew things that seemed important for a future woman like me to know, things like the intricacies of love and the mysteries of lying in bed with a man.

Aunt Sparkle wasn't the only member of my family in the music business, of course, but she looked the part more than the rest of us. Yes, 4 The Cause had toured all over Europe, and my cousins and I had a blast attending the Stellar Awards and touring with Raven-Symoné in 1996. And as a well-respected guitarist in the deep bench of Chicago talent, Dad gigged all around playing everything from funk and R&B to gospel, jazz, and hip-hop, though he made his most regular paychecks playing for gospel artists at church productions. But it was Aunt Sparkle who shined like new money as her star continued to rise in the R&B universe.

She was a credited background vocalist on Aaliyah's 1994 double-platinum debut album, *Age Ain't Nothing but a Number*, produced by R. Kelly, who, by then, was killing the R&B game on the international stage. And two years later, Sparkle became R. Kelly's next musical protégé in the process of signing with his newly incorporated Rockland Records. (Sparkle's self-titled album debuted in 1998 and went platinum.)

At twelve, I didn't know much about the business side of my own group's recording contract much less Sparkle's music deal. I was just excited...for all of us. As a kid musician and favorite niece of my favorite aunt, I had a glimpse at the adult world of entertainment. But I was still very much a kid, and when I wasn't touring with my group, I was content to shoot hoops and hang with my junior high friends. I knew that I was a part of a talented musical family, of course, and that we all wanted to follow our gifts and talents wherever they would lead us. But the most important thing was that I felt loved and supported by them, especially Aunt Sparkle.

* * *

It was the late fall or early winter of 1996 when Aunt Sparkle cheered on my cousins and me at our 4 The Cause concert for the local Chicago crowd. She brought a guest: R. Kelly.

I had no way of knowing how Aunt Sparkle's unexpected guest would make my preteen life in Chicago and my musical aspirations clash and ultimately cancel each other out. I was just happy to take the stage in Chicago and amazed to meet R. Kelly when I got offstage! R. Kelly, a bona fide star. R. Kelly, who was everywhere and loved by everyone, especially here in Chicago. Of course I knew his music. Of course I admired him. *Everyone* did. I was excited to spot him at a Fred Hammond gospel concert at my church once, but this was on another level. Not only was Aunt Sparkle R. Kelly's protégée, but now *he* was my group's newest and most famous fan!

I know that some folks feel otherwise, but, even now, I believe that Sparkle's initial intention in introducing R. Kelly to my family came from a place of wanting to see all of us win like she was. And in Chicago in 1996, as a musical talent in a crowded field of hopefuls, you wanted to get as close to him as you could. I'm sure that's one reason why she connected to him as she did. He was a hitmaker; he knew the sound folks couldn't get enough of. And he was still here in Chicago making music when lots of folks would have set up shop in New York City or LA. It was like Chi-town, my city, was his muse.

I wasn't thinking about any of that, though. I was just starstruck, excited that my aunt was starting a new career and amazed that this artist I was inspired by was acknowledging me. He said he was wowed by us and especially wowed by me as the youngest and smallest member of the group. He made a point of singling me out, complimenting me on my stage presence and giving me constructive criticism about how to handle myself as a performer. He made me feel seen and respected as an artist, something I so wanted to be. And just when I thought things couldn't get better, he decided to treat my family to a meal at Cheesecake Factory.

I can no longer remember all that we talked about at dinner, but it was the beginning of getting to know R. Kelly the star as Robert Kelly the man. Since Aunt Sparkle was working on music at Robert's studio, I started tagging along and hanging around the studio too. I loved soaking up the energy; it made me that much more excited about my own dreams of being a singer and rapper. At some point during those early days—maybe it was even at our Cheesecake Factory dinner—Robert learned that my dad was a great guitarist. So Robert asked Dad to become a studio musician for him. Although my dad is credited on several R. Kelly albums, he never played onstage with Robert; he would just go to the studio and lay tracks to inspire Robert in his songwriting. When Dad went to play music, I took those opportunities to join him at the studio.

It felt great to be around Robert and witness his talent firsthand. And I was also tickled to have a celebrity friend. In addition to the time I spent at the studio, I would also go with Aunt Sparkle or my parents to watch him play basketball with his friends or employees when he'd rent out Hoops The Gym in Chicago's West Loop neighborhood. Then he would take all of us to the Rock'n'Roll McDonald's on North Clark Street or the Cheesecake Factory on North Michigan. Hanging out with Robert was fun, and because he was famous, it was like I was brushed by greatness. Of course, I had met folks who were famous in other countries when I toured with 4 The Cause. And our fans in those countries screamed for our group, which made *me* feel famous. So, to an extent, I was accustomed to meeting people in the music industry, both here and abroad. But this was the first time I was connected to a huge celebrity I personally looked up to, right here at home. It felt terrific, like my whole family was on the come-up.

It was a couple of months into my new friendship with Robert, and I was at Aunt Sparkle's apartment when she said, "Hey, Chon, the next time we're at the studio, you should ask Robert to be your godfather."

I turned her words over in my mind. "Yeah, that's actually a great idea because that'll make me closer to him." I thought it would be more of a good thing, which seemed great to me. But since I had to make this request for myself, I felt nervous about it. Aunt Sparkle explained that I should sit on his lap and rub his head while I asked him to be my godfather. This instruction seemed sort of weird since I hadn't sat on his lap before, but I didn't question it.

The next time I was at the studio with her, I went into his office and did exactly what she told me to do. I was surprised that sitting on his lap created a feeling in me that was beyond the friendship we'd been cultivating. *Is this okay to do?* Some part of me wondered why it didn't feel like sitting on Mom's lap or even Dad's.

Robert stayed put and acted normal. Then he looked up at me, his smile broad and warm. "Yes."

"Wow!" I smiled. I didn't know what I had been expecting, but it seemed almost too easy. "Cool!" My heart felt happy. Now *I* was a part of *his* family.

When I shared the news of my change in status with my parents, they noted that I already had godparents, but they said this was great. To my mind, they knew that I was also into basketball and music, like Robert was, so they could see that we had meaningful things in common. Robert had visited our church and had given his life to Christ, so as far as I knew, no one was holding the old rumors about him liking teenage girls against him.

Hanging at my mom's parents' house was always a good time. Sundays and holidays were the days when *everyone* came over. My aunts and uncles liked to call my grandparents' house "the shelter" because it was the spot where you could come empty-handed and without having called to announce your arrival, and the house would be full of family, good food, and lots of conversation. Sometimes Aunt Sparkle would walk in late saying her ears were burning so bad that she just *had* to come by and see what folks were gossiping about her. Aunt Sparkle wasn't wrong; everyone and everything was fair game to discuss in my grandparents' den. And you could be talked about whether you were there to defend yourself or not. The room, full of too much furniture and folks over the age of nineteen, was where everyone got caught up on the career moves and romantic lives of everyone else while hoping that they wouldn't land in the hot seat.

Since I was a kid, my presence wasn't immediately shooed away, but I knew—like my cousins did—that we were supposed to keep it moving through the den. Sure, we could walk in and out on the way to the kitchen or bathroom, but if we kids wanted to eavesdrop on the conversation, we had to plant ourselves in the living room, which was right next to the den. There, we'd hear everything that was being said without being seen. And to make it look like we weren't doing what we were doing, we'd turn on the TV to a kids' show and maybe chat mindlessly with another cousin. If I noticed that the topic of conversation in the den turned to music and career stuff, I'd be ear hustling, silently scrutinizing who said what and why.

Before my connection to Robert became a sore spot for our family, our R. Kelly association was a frequent topic of conversation in the den. Sitting in the room with my mom and dad were Mom's siblings: Aunt Sparkle, Aunt Charlotte, Uncle Bennie, and Uncle Kook (who was the manager of 4 The Cause, my group with my cousins). When Robert's name entered their spirited chitchat, I could tell their words weren't meant for young ears, so mine immediately perked up from the living room.

"People always worried about who R. Kelly's sleeping with. Like it's their business. They should worry about their own raggedy love lives. He's got a *wife*, for God's sakes," Aunt Charlotte huffed.

"Didn't he get saved?" Mom chimed in.

"Didn't we *all*, Valerie?" Aunt Sparkle sounded amused.

"Well then," Mom said. "'Let he who is without sin cast the first stone' is all I gotta say about that. If God forgives and forgets, then why should anybody bring up rumors?"

"That's my point!" Aunt Charlotte responded.

Aunt Sparkle laughed. "Not exactly, Charlotte, but okay! Valerie, I think we're all grown enough to know that getting saved and staying saved are two very different things." She chuckled again. "But you're right that they're rumors."

"This industry is full of haters." Uncle Kook spoke with authority. "I'm sure R. Kelly's got plenty!"

Uncle Bennie's laugh boomed. "What'd they say about crabs in a barrel? That's how folks are. Especially if they ain't on the gravy train!"

"Say *that*!" Aunt Charlotte piped up. "But that man has shown our family nothing but love, and it's surely not because y'all are rich, famous, or powerful!"

"Speak for yourself!" Aunt Sparkle joked.

"Oh, we forgot! Stephanie has *already* arrived!" Mom was always quick with her replies. She chuckled. "But seriously, what's wrong with being on the gravy train?"

The room went silent, and my stomach clenched from nervousness. *Did Mom just say that out loud? Is that really how she feels?*

Then Mom laughed at her own question, and the rest of them joined in.

"Girl, I thought you were trippin' for a minute!" Aunt Sparkle responded. "Look, I know that Robert is a lotta things, but one of those things is a musical genius who's making bank!"

"I tell you what. I don't care if R. Kelly wipes his ass with hundred-dollar bills, just as long as he ain't handin' my family no shit sandwich! Then he'll have to deal with *me*. So, handle your business, fam, and I'll deal with the rest." Uncle Bennie responded more loudly than the others.

Everyone was quiet. I guess they were digesting his meaning like I was.

Dad broke the silence. "Rob runs this town for sure." His voice was gravel.

"More than this *town*, Greg," Aunt Sparkle answered. "You know that like I do. That's why I *had* to put you on!"

"Thank you."

"Of course. How could I keep my good fortune all to myself?"

Someone snapped to punctuate Aunt Sparkle's words.

"I mean, Robert's like y'all's age and he's already a legend!" Aunt Sparkle continued her thought.

"And his nose ain't stuck up in the clouds either," Aunt Charlotte added.

"It's really not," Mom agreed. "Look, I was shocked when he became Reshona's godfather. I just didn't see that coming."

"But he's been a blessing to us," Dad finished Mom's thought. "To our whole family. We're blessed to be on his short list of important people. I don't even know how that happened."

"That's what I'm *saying*, Greg. I'm not just singing background anymore. I'll have my own album on his label. And now that you're playing with him and getting your name out there in some different circles, it's like our family is finally building our own musical empire!"

"What do you think *I've* been doing?" Uncle Kook's voice was full of fake offense.

"R. Kelly has made *us* his family. And I'm grateful!" Mom's voice dripped with the blood of Jesus. She clapped her hands. "That's God! I don't care what *nobody* says!"

"Look, Valerie, before you start catchin' the Holy Ghost," Aunt Sparkle huffed, "let me just say this. Robert is nobody's Jesus Jr., okay? God knows this business has way more Satans than saints. But I'm happy Chon has become like a daughter to Robert, because he does know how to take care of his kids. And Greg and Kook know how this business chews folks up and spits them out with a quickness. I'm sure Robert has chewed up some folks, too, but having the biggest dog in your corner is what you want."

Aunt Sparkle paused. I hung on to her warning as much as everyone in the den. "Robert Sylvester Kelly is a genius whose song catalog is like a whole damn bank. So, for as long as he's churning out the hits everybody wants to bump and grind to, we'd be stupid to pick a fight with him. If he wants us to be his family, we can do that! And if we get blessed with some coins, hit songs, fame, or whatever else, I'm not mad at that either. None of us should be. Let God worry about Robert's soul, Valerie. But I know God can use *anyone* to bless us, so I'll take it!"

Aunt Sparkle's words rang in my ears. I did feel blessed. And her advice seemed sound. I couldn't think of one good reason why any of us would want to pick a fight with Robert. Having him as my godfather—and his wife, Andrea, as my godmother by extension—made me their family and expanded my footprint tremendously. I had free rein and could hang out with Robert at the studio even more, sometimes with Aunt Sparkle, sometimes with Dad, or sometimes by myself. My world was already built on the firm foundation of a family who held my dreams like stars in the sky. Now it felt like I could grab hold of those stars and let them glisten in my hands.

CHAPTER 2

CATCHING FEELINGS

A FEW MONTHS INTO being twelve, I was playing in an AAU basketball game when my first period caught me by surprise. Initially, I was embarrassed, thinking I hadn't wiped well. But when Mom picked me up and we made what I thought would be a pit stop at Granny's house, Granny stepped in like she had been waiting her whole life for this.

"Do you have cramps, Reshona?" Mom seemed caught off guard by my news and at a loss about what to do.

Granny left the room and walked into the bathroom.

"I don't *think* so." I wasn't sure what cramps felt like. "I mean, it felt like, I don't know, a little weird feeling and then I thought I had an accident. It felt like I couldn't help it." I hunched my shoulders.

"Well, praise be!" Granny's voice returned to the room before her body did. She was holding a value-sized bottle of Massengill feminine wash. "Now that you're a little lady, Reshona, you have to keep yourself very fresh and clean." She shook the Massengill in her hand. "Valerie, the child needs some pads. Go into that hall closet where I keep my extra supplies and things and grab me a maxi pad and a pair of dark blue or red panties. Not white."

Mom's face was stamped with surprise. "I didn't think you needed pads anymore, Ma."

"I've got daughters, nieces, and now *granddaughters* who might need them." She nodded and smiled at me. "Things happen, Valerie. Can you please just get the panties and four pads so she can put one in her school backpack and have two for tonight?" Granny shook her head.

Mom disappeared into the back of the house.

Granny chatted about the miracle of being able to bring forth new life. I squinted because I didn't get it, and because I felt another one of those weird feelings deep inside, below my belly button. I had never thought much about there being anything else inside of me other than my bladder, but I knew this wasn't urine even though I was wetting myself. And now Granny had her arms on my shoulders, rocking herself and me, her smile full of awe for the wonders of God.

My face must have been full of confusion when Mom returned, four thick maxi pads flapping in her hands. "She means that you can get pregnant, Reshona, that your body is able to, because you got your period." Mom's face was pressed into a light frown.

I answered her frown with my own. *That* was something light-years from my mind. Judging from Mom's face, that made two of us.

"Yes. Reshona, once God blesses you with a *good* God-fearing man to be your husband and your family's provider, then you'll surely be blessed to have babies." Granny smiled. "But until that happy day, let's get you cleaned up."

Granny led me to her bathroom, closed the door, and waited. I had been using the bathroom by myself for years, so I waited too. "Reshona, I forgot to tell Valerie to get you a washcloth. Go get one, please. Not white. And bring the Woolite, too. You'll need to sponge out those soiled panties." Granny shooed me away with her hand and sat on the edge of the bathtub.

I started running but, feeling another weird feeling, I slowed down. I didn't know what I'd find in my underwear, and the idea that Granny was going to find out when I did made me hot with embarrassment.

Returning to the bathroom with washcloth and Woolite in hand, I found Granny humming a hymn. "Don't be nervous, baby. I went through this with each of my three daughters. It's something that happens to all girls at some point. And today is your day! Now, let's get out of those clothes so you can take a shower."

When Granny saw me hesitate at her instruction, she turned to give me privacy until I was behind her frosted shower curtain. I wondered how much she could see of me, but she acted like it was normal for her to be in the bathroom with me as I stood naked in the shower. Granny coached me through how to clean myself from top to bottom, giving me an especially detailed play-by-play on how to manage my vaginal hygiene.

When it was time to get out, she held out a bath towel and I was only too happy to wrap myself in it. "Now you're gonna handwash these in a moment." She motioned toward my soiled underwear staring up at me from the bathroom sink, which was *not* where I had left them. I was embarrassed all over again.

"Step into your clean panties, Reshona, and pull them up to your knees."

I readjusted my towel so it wouldn't fall.

"My grandma used to call them step-ins since you step into them." Granny chuckled at the memory. "Okay, good, Reshona. Now watch what I do." She pulled a long strip off the underside of the pad that I hadn't even realized was there. "Now, be careful to hold the pad by the sides to keep it clean. You don't want any dirt getting inside of you."

I had just taken a shower and washed myself according to Granny's step-by-step instructions, so I couldn't imagine I had any dirt on my hands. I thought about all the times I had run in from playing basketball or football and quickly washed my hands before going to the bathroom without giving a thought to the dirt and sweat on my skin before wiping myself. *Had I been contaminating myself without even realizing it?* I didn't want to ask Granny. I feared that her answer would be yes and that she'd have lots more instructions on how to use the bathroom. "Okay." I took the pad from her, taking care to hold it as she was.

"Now, press it into your underwear so it sticks, Reshona."

I was holding my bath towel with my left hand and the pad with my right. I didn't have an extra hand to press the pad into my panties. I clamped my left underarm tight up against my body and let go of the towel with my hand. My hands fumbling with the pad, I felt my towel slipping off my body. I froze.

"It's okay, baby."

I kept trying to protect my modesty.

"Okay, Reshona. Let me just keep that up for you." Granny held up my towel and I pressed the pad into my panties. She didn't say anything when my fingers touched the center of it by mistake, though I heard her make a small gasp. "Okay, good. Now scoot your panties all the way up."

I did. Granny handed my falling towel back to me and turned her back. She was studying my soiled panties in the sink. I had forgotten about those. Did she really expect me to wash them and hold up my towel, too?

"Would you like a robe to wear, Reshona?"

"Yes. Please!"

"Valerie, please grab this child my extra robe—the terry-cloth one—that's on the hook on the door of my second closet. It might be under a few things. Just look for it."

When Mom returned with the robe, I put it on over the towel, tying it tight. Granny completed my tutorial with Mom standing in the doorway of the bathroom. I couldn't understand why she needed to be there too, but since Granny had talked me through my shower, I decided to leave that question alone.

From that point on, I knew exactly what to do, and thankfully, I was trusted to manage it on my own. Mom even bought me my own box of pads. I just had to let her know when I needed more. (I didn't learn about the existence of tampons for several more years.) I felt different. More feminine somehow. I started to notice how girls at school dressed and wore their hair so I could take pointers on how to represent myself as the adolescent girl I now knew myself to be.

These experiences quickly found their place in my future-woman tool kit, right alongside the suggestive '90s lyrics penned by my godfather and his contemporaries and Aunt Sparkle's equally spicy stories of her romantic adventures.

Aunt Sparkle had already shared with me that she had been intimate with Robert. I was thirteen years old when she asked if he had gotten me something for Christmas. Though I had been enjoying the perks of being Robert's goddaughter—playing basketball on reserved courts, dining at Cheesecake Factory for no reason at all, and especially hanging with him at the studio—I hadn't thought much about the fact that he didn't get me a present until Aunt Sparkle asked. "No," I answered, my voice flat.

"Oh." Aunt Sparkle's voice was nonchalant. She looked down at her arm and slipped on a chunky silver bracelet with a big *G* on it. Then she ran her finger along the *G*.

I watched as her finger traced the letter over and over. "Did he get *you* something?" I asked. I hadn't cared one second before, and part of me still didn't. But now a part of me did.

"Yes, Chon!" Aunt Sparkle's eyes shined. "He got me *this*!" Her mouth pulled into a demure smile, she stuck out her arm so I could get a good look at the bracelet she had been playing with. "Gucci!" She answered the question I didn't ask.

"Oh wow." I stared. "It's pretty."

"Isn't it?" Aunt Sparkle admired it again.

I couldn't think of anything else to say. The silence between us felt strange. *I* felt strange. *Why did she ask me that? And why do I feel bad all of a sudden?* I couldn't figure out why she chose that way to tell me what he had gotten her or why I felt weird. I didn't realize it was the stirrings of jealousy.

I can't remember which crush came first, Romiel or Jonathan. But since I didn't really know how to act around them, I just made sure I played basketball, football, or whatever the boys were playing so I could be around them in my free time. And once one of them and

I established that we both liked each other, we'd walk home from school together, sometimes stopping to get a daily double at the local McDonald's, before giving each other a goodbye hug.

Whereas I never seemed to know what to discuss with Jonathan and had resorted to playfighting with Romiel when we were crushing on each other, I never had a problem engaging in long and thoughtful conversations with Robert.

Despite the temporary weirdness with Aunt Sparkle, I had fun with Robert. He was interested in what I was interested in, and he didn't mind talking basketball or music for as long as I wanted to. With him on his cell and me on my home phone—I had my own phone line that rang only in my room—we recounted the highlights of our days. He always had an endless string of questions about my family and friends, and he seemed to genuinely value my opinions.

When I was around Robert, I started feeling little tingles, almost like butterflies, when he would grab my head and kiss me on the forehead or when the two of us were watching a movie together at the studio. It felt exhilarating. As I peppered him with questions about his life during our phone conversations—questions that he seemed all too willing to answer—I realized that I was nursing a crush that felt altogether new. Better than my awkward kiddie crushes, this was also more meaningful than a celebrity crush because I was getting to know the person behind the R. Kelly persona. I began to look forward to our rambling phone conversations. Then, when I was at the studio one day, Robert hugged me a little too long and a little too tight. And my newly teenage body felt something had changed between us.

From that point forward, our phone conversations took on another dimension. I remember when, early on, I was lounging on my twin bed in the late afternoon. I had already finished my homework and was listening to music on my black stereo set in the corner of my room. I pulled off my jeans so I could hang out in my bed until Mom called me for dinner. I grabbed my red cordless phone, and it lit up as I dialed Robert's cell phone number. As we chitchatted—my feet pushed under the jumble of covers on my bed and my knees tucked under my chin—I imagined that my wall posters of Foxy Brown, 702, and especially Usher were all eavesdropping on my conversation with Robert.

"What do you have on right now?" Robert's voice sounded different.

I stopped looking at Usher and glanced down at myself. "Drawers and a T-shirt." My reply was quick and unrehearsed.

He corrected me. "Don't say it like that. That's not attractive. Say 'panties and a T-shirt.'"

"Um, panties and a T-shirt," I repeated.

"Better." Robert's voice was thick. He cleared his throat. "I *like* that..."

With my phone cradled against my ear, Robert's loud, irregular breathing penetrated my brain. I thought to ask him if he was okay but stopped myself. Thankful that I was the only one with my phone line and that my parents were equally busy talking on their home phone line, I realized that my question was dumb. I looked down at my drawers—*panties* now—marveling at their transformation. The idea that I could say a word that Robert found attractive or unattractive amazed me. My first lesson about what Robert liked felt as if I had cracked open the lid to Pandora's box. I had little idea what could open it wider, but the cocktail of hormones that swirled around inside of me made me wonder. Though I suspected that Aunt Sparkle might know, something about this felt private, like I was being drawn into a secret.

Keeping secrets for Robert was another of his lessons.

I wasn't fourteen yet when I found myself wading into the murky waters of amorous entanglements and competing secrets. The phone conversations between Robert and me still began with the regular chatter about how we spent our days, but it wouldn't take too long before he steered us further away from the familiar and into uncharted territory.

"Be ready to talk that shit for Daddy." Robert's words were a command and an invitation.

"Okay."

"You know your words make me feel stuff, Sho? Can you guess where my hand is?"

"Are you touching your chest?"

"Keep going."

"Your belly button?"

"Closer."

"Are you touching *yourself*?"

"Tell me what I'm touching."

He took me on a tour of himself: what he was wearing, and how he was touching himself. His voice husky with anticipation, he navigated me through the same. "How do your nipples feel? Are they hard?"

"They're regular. No, I guess."

"Then squeeze them. Roll them between your fingers."

At his direction, I began to explore my budding body.

"I bet they're hard now."

"Yes."

Robert had already told me that our special conversations were just between us. I felt conflicted about the secrecy of our exchanges but blown away that he knew things about my body that I didn't. I didn't want anything bad to happen to him or me if anyone found out about them, so I quickly switched into protective mode and stayed quiet.

This was how Robert introduced me to the world of phone sex. His commanding voice instructed me on how to awaken my own sexual response, which was unexpected for me, but he seemed to know it was there. With a grown man's confidence, he reassured me that what we were doing was natural and that my body wanted it as much as his. Even as our secrets multiplied, the emotions that twisted around my heart and burned within me made me desperate to believe him. After all, how could my body do all of this? I had just turned fourteen.

I kept my deepening but muddled feelings to myself, my mind barely comprehending the messiness of the whole situation. While I was beginning to crave more alone time with Robert, I was also growing in my love and admiration for his wife, Andrea, as my godmother. An accomplished dancer in her own right, Andrea was beautiful and elegant, and never hesitated to indulge our shared love of shopping and eating out. We'd make a day of it at Water Tower Place on Chicago's Magnificent Mile: me getting my Tommy Hilfiger fix and her buying a new leotard or specialty dance item before we stopped for a decadent drink at Starbucks, a place she put me on to. Then we'd bond over a chick flick at the movie theater or come back to their home and watch a rom-com in their TV room, complete with sparkling apple cider and Andrea's special spaghetti, as a kickoff to an impromptu sleepover.

Andrea also shared her beauty regimen, explaining that what she ate was even more important than the cosmetics she sometimes wore. I learned that she chose not to eat red meat to promote optimal health. Her glowing skin was a ringing endorsement, and at fourteen, I stopped eating it too. These were genuine moments for us; I looked up to her as a woman who was following her professional passions while also being a good mother. But a part of me felt like an understudy of who she was. I watched how she maneuvered with Robert and seemed to accept his lifestyle, wondering how I would feel if I ever got top billing in Robert's life.

Aunt Sparkle wasn't a safe confidante for my questions because of her own entanglement with Robert. My pangs of jealousy were real. When she dropped sexual tidbits, her loaded statements seemed to draw dotted lines of comparison between his treatment of her as his musical protégée and of me as his goddaughter. And I knew each of our official relationships had an unspoken counterpart, which for Robert included being a married man. But it was hard for me to grasp how many lines had been crossed since those lines seemed not to exist for Robert. That made me willing to let them blur, too. Of course, he had forbidden me from telling Aunt Sparkle or anyone about me "talking shit for Daddy" because our secret was something others wouldn't understand. With the gnawing feeling that Aunt Sparkle was my competition for Robert's heart, I took his word for it.

"Chon, can you keep a secret?" Aunt Sparkle shared lots of things, but she didn't often say that what she shared with me was a secret, so I perked up.

"For sure!" I was at her apartment, watching her try on her clothes. She'd try on an outfit and then say that too many people had seen her wear it before, or that it wasn't in style anymore and she needed to buy some new things. But it all looked great to me. Everything was silky, shiny, skintight, or short. And on her slim but shapely frame, everything made her look like a star. I said as much.

"Thanks, Chon!" She blew a kiss through the air that landed on my nose. "But let me tell you my secret!" She sat down beside me on her bed so we could be at eye level. "I have a boyfriend!"

"Oh wow!" She sounded excited, so I felt excited for her.

"I'll tell you who, but you have to *promise* to keep it a secret."

"Okay, who?" Of course I wouldn't tell. Who would I tell, anyway?

"Okay!" Aunt Sparkle's face lit up before she said his name. "He's a producer and songwriter. His name is Steve Huff!"

I smiled. I felt happy for her. I had no idea who Steve Huff was, but it was clear that Aunt Sparkle did and that she was glad to have him as her boyfriend.

"Do you *love* him or *like* him?" That felt like a good, girlfriendy kind of question to ask.

Aunt Sparkle laughed. "What do *you* know about loving and liking men?" She shook her head and laughed again. "I think I could love him, Chon. Maybe even soon, I don't know." Aunt Sparkle looked dreamy for a moment. "But I'm serious about keeping this a top-notch secret, especially from Robert."

"Okay."

"I'm serious, Chon. Steve and Robert practically hate each other. If Robert finds out, he'll tank me."

I must've looked puzzled.

"He'll ruin my career, Chon. Do you understand? I mean, my personal business is *not* his business. We're just in business together. That's all. But he can mess things up for me. That's why I don't need him up in my shit. You understand?"

"Okay."

She opened her eyes wide at me.

"Yes, I understand." I had no desire to share her news, and there was no one to share it with anyway, so it was my full intention to do what Aunt Sparkle asked of me.

* * *

At some point, Aunt Sparkle started questioning me about my conversations with Robert. She wasn't asking about what *I* discussed with him, only whether he said anything about *her*. Did he ask about her romantic relationships? My answer was always no... until he did.

I was fourteen and a half and Aunt Sparkle's debut album on Robert's new label had just dropped. One day when I was at the studio, Robert came into the room with me. The studio was a maze of dark, windowless rooms, some with control panels and recording booths. Others were black boxes full of sofas, blow-up mattresses, massage tables, and dozens of framed platinum records.

Robert closed the door and stood in front of it. I craned my neck to look at him from my seat on the couch. "I need to ask you a question, and I need you to be honest with me." His voice was measured, but no-nonsense.

"Okay," I answered, but inside, I turned to jelly. I felt like I knew what he was going to ask, and I hoped he wouldn't because Aunt Sparkle told me not to tell him. But I didn't feel that I could lie to him either. He was my godfather and the person I most wanted to please. I also knew he had authority over me.

Robert stepped closer, his hand still on the doorknob. I pressed my body into the couch, hoping I'd disappear.

"Does Sparkle have a boyfriend?"

"Yes." He drilled holes into my brain with his stare. I was sure he could see everything I was thinking.

"Well, do you know who it is?"

"Yes." I knew it was too little of an answer.

"What's his *name*?" he growled, his voice as hard as his eyes.

"Steve Huff," I whispered.

"I fucking *knew* it! I fucking *knew* it!" Robert's voice felt like hot venom spewing down on me.

I was sitting there squirming, knowing that Robert was as angry as Aunt Sparkle said he would be and that she would be mad at me, too. I didn't know what to do. I don't know what Robert and Aunt Sparkle discussed after that, but it became painfully clear to me that my revelation had, in fact, jeopardized her music career like she said it would. They started arguing at the studio and their business relationship was completely toxic after that. All this happened when she was filming videos for her first songs to be released as singles. Yes, her album went platinum, but her time with Robert was basically over. I don't know how long it took for it to officially end or what the terms were for them to part ways, but it definitely ended. Guilt made my ears perk up to the gossipy tidbits I overheard at the studio and my mom's side of several phone conversations I ear hustled at home, so I knew Aunt Sparkle blamed me for what happened.

Of course, I was still Robert's goddaughter, and Dad was a session musician for him, so I was still around. But now Aunt Sparkle wasn't. And just like that, my unsupervised time with Robert doubled. Now our secret conversations could happen in person.

At the risk of getting ahead of myself, I want to share three quick thoughts. One: I hope you don't snap the book shut now and rush to spill the tea on social media about how I have an effed-up family. This shit's complicated and lots of folks have messy families, maybe including yours.

Two: I am a mother, a daughter, a sister, a niece, a coworker, and a Black woman in America trying to be whole. I'm choosing to be transparent, not to be someone's punch line or punching bag, but to try to heal. We've all got to heal from one thing or another; maybe there's something in my story that will help you.

Three, and this is big: I don't hate Aunt Sparkle. I love her. She was and still is a talented and beautiful woman. I appreciate that she always saw my gifts and talents and wanted me to soar in the music industry. Those good intentions notwithstanding, not every choice was good. And sometimes she—like many—may not have been clear about her intentions. I also know that the crap that happened between Sparkle and Robert wasn't "my fault." I was a child entrusted with information I shouldn't have been given (I'll elaborate further later). Hindsight is 20/20. But we live going forward, not backward. So, left to my own devices, I was about to jump from a frying pan into a fire.

CHAPTER 3

NEVER HAVE I EVER

SEVENTH GRADE WAS A tale of two Reshonas. I wasn't touring with 4 The Cause, so I was able to trade in the gigs, practice, and disruptive—though fun—European tours for all the trimmings at Emerson Junior High School. From science projects and mystery meat in the cafeteria to cringey school dances, my basketball team's winning streak, and the whirlwind of my best friends' crushes. Everything was normal...mostly. Good even. Except that I didn't talk about *my* crush. And my sleepovers were strictly for the other Reshona.

My whole school knew about my celebrity godfather. Chi-town, the city of broad shoulders, was known for its wicked winds, deep-dish pizza, and R. Kelly. Why would I keep my connection to Robert a secret? I was only too happy to have his thundering voice cheering me on at my basketball games alongside Mom's, Dad's, and lil Greg's. I was already a solid B+ student admired for my skill on the basketball court and well liked for my fun personality. The addition of Robert to all of that just heightened my appeal. And who would say no to a little more junior high popularity? I surely didn't.

Sometimes I hung out with friends after school, and several times a week, I'd hop the train to Robert's Chicago Trax studio. There, I'd do my homework and then walk around, listen to the music being developed by Robert and his bevy of musicians, and ask Robert's runner to get me my favorite snack to eat: a twice-baked potato from a little spot near the studio. Whenever my dad had a session at Robert's studio, I'd tag along then, too, and casually mention I was staying for the weekend to spend time with my godmother, Andrea, and help her with her and Robert's firstborn daughter. I can't remember ever being told no.

In public, I was the perfect goddaughter. But in private, Robert called me his heaven-sent secret lover. Feeling needed by him was the lure.

Even though I had heard Aunt Sparkle's stories of her own sexual relationships with Robert and her various boyfriends, I didn't understand what my own romantic feelings or sexual desires would feel like, or how my heart could make my body want things and my mind believe things that Robert did and said. Sure, Usher was my celebrity crush, but he lived in my teenage daydreams (except the one time I met him at Robert's studio and Robert said he was jealous, when all I did was smile at Usher and gush about loving his music).

Robert was *real.*

With Robert's sure hand steadying my pubescent body, I became intoxicated with the rush of thoughts, feelings, and experiences I had with him. I didn't know he was studying me when he touched me, that all his words were spoken with intent and every hurdle I bounded over—his hand clutching mine—was designed to make me invested in what I now know was abuse. At the time, it didn't feel like abuse. I had no idea that he had hastened my sexual awakening and weaponized my teenage gullibility. Being Robert's secret lover was delicious, even though it was a little dangerous. My heart was exploding in my chest. My body felt *good*, and I believed those thrills and shivers could only come from him. But I don't care how good it might have felt, a fourteen-year-old girl should *not* be turned out by a thirty-one-year-old man. Full stop. My teen mind was as scrambled about this issue as it could be. When your body starts to have sexual feelings and desires, it seems like whoever can make you feel good is the right person for you, no matter their age. But the man who said age ain't nothing but a number lied.

Moments of intimacy felt special, in the beginning. Robert would lay his head on my chest and tell me things. Even more than sexual ecstasy, what I most craved was being Robert's confidante, his special secret jewel, his soft place to land. In the quiet, when it was him sharing difficult stories from his childhood or what was bothering him with his musicians or his family, I believed that our relationship was right. I believed that I was what he needed.

"You know what you are, Sho? You know what you are to me?"

"No."

"You're my angel. God *sent* you to me."

"You think so?"

"I *know* so. 'Cause you don't judge me. You accept me for who I am."

My smile was loud enough for Robert to hear. He cocked his head and poked out his lips so I could kiss them. I did.

"These haters out here wouldn't understand what we got. They don't want me to have you. They want me all fucked up in my mental."

I frowned. "Are you?" I didn't know what he would say, but the warmth that spread through me like maple syrup on pancakes made me want to hear whatever he wanted to say. In that moment, I was his safe place, and that felt good.

"Not now. Not anymore. Not with you, baby." His voice was just a whisper, but it set off fireworks inside of me.

Robert ran his thumbs over his eyebrows and then over mine. His action, a secret sign of love for me that he'd do whenever he was onstage, sent a wave of contentment through me. My mind turned over this complicated and beautiful feeling of being needed by a man so rich and so powerful. So loved by millions of people. But *he* needed *me*.

"Will you always be here for me, Sho?"

His words felt heavy. *What would "always" look like? Would I* always *be a secret?* His question made my swirl of thoughts and feelings a little more complicated and less beautiful. "Yeah, I guess so."

Then he lifted his head up. "Damn, Sho." He looked me square in the eye and held the stare until I had to look away. "I just opened up my whole fucking heart to you and that's what you say? 'I guess so'? What the fuck, Sho! I mean, God *sent* you to me. I just said it. Are you gonna be less than the angel you're supposed to be?"

I felt tears gathering in the corners of my eyes. I didn't know how to answer him right, but what I said was clearly more wrong than I imagined.

He took my silence as an opportunity to answer the question in my mind. He lifted his head so I could see his eyes, which I was surprised to see glistening like mine. "You know, you confuse me sometimes, Sho. I mean, you understand me on a level that is beyond anybody and anything I've ever experienced. You so far beyond grown-ass women..." His voice trailed off and he shook his head. "I don't know *what* God gave you for *me*. I mean, your agape love and bulletproof loyalty. It's like you got *everything* for me, Sho!

I don't hardly understand it! Maybe you don't either. But I love you *deep*."

His lips brushed mine. I felt so full that I thought I might burst. And yet, I wanted more.

"Do you love me, Sho?"

I nodded violently. I couldn't trust myself to speak.

He pulled up one corner of his lips into a smile. "I can't hear you." He drank my immature nipple into his mouth like a baby hungry for milk. My body was aflame. Then he stopped. "The answer is yes, Sho. Your answer to me is *always* yes."

"Yes," I whispered.

"Yes, *what*?"

"Yes, Robert?" We were the only two people in the room. I was afraid I was messing up again.

"Call me Daddy."

The word clanged around in my head and dumped ice water on the flames that had threatened to consume me only a moment before. *Daddy?!* I called my father Daddy. I loved my daddy, but I didn't lie down naked with him and please him like I did with Robert.

"Did you hear me, Sho?"

"Yes."

"Yes, *what*?"

"But I call my dad—"

"Are you fucking kidding me right now? Are you bringing another *man* into my bed?"

"No, Robert. I mean—"

"Well, what do you want to call me?"

Robert. But I knew that was the wrong answer.

"Tell me."

"I don't know." I lowered my head, ashamed.

"You *should*. Because I already told you."

Robert's breath was hot on my face. I wanted to turn my face away from him, but I knew that would make him angry.

"What we have is *special*, Sho. If you love me like I love you, then you need to do what I say. Because *I* love you so hard it hurts, baby. And *I* can protect you. Do you understand?"

"Yes, Daddy." It felt like my brain turned on a white noise machine just as a new wave of excitement moved through Robert's body. It was time for me to be his angel, again.

It was a tall order. Being Robert's angel, Robert's best girl, Robert's sexual fix *and* creative inspiration meant I was only as good as *Robert* said I was, only as good as my ability and willingness to love him the way he wanted me to. But every time I arrived at some new magical plane of existence that was so special and so right, then he had to test it and stretch it somehow. Being Robert's lover meant I kept having to become more of what *he* wanted me to be. Yes, I was the best thing, but never enough.

"It's time for the next level, baby."

I had been studying the hangnail on my left thumb and resisting the urge to chew on it in front of Robert when he spoke. I looked up.

"You heard me, Sho?"

Of course. We're the only ones in here. I looked down so I could roll my eyes without him seeing me do it. *Next level?* Even in the dim light of the studio room that had become our secret hiding place whenever I was there, Robert's eyes shined like crude-oil slicks floating atop a midnight-blue ocean. I knew that look. It made me sick. The hairs on my body stood up.

"We *overdue*!" Robert's voice quivered with excitement. He had been getting bored with me, with us. His blue-black eyes told me he was about to change all that. But I didn't want any more changes. What part of my body was going to be pressed into service of his latest fetish? Would it be my ears? My nose? Something else? I felt like every part of me had to be ready for Robert's next level.

I started chewing on my hangnail. I didn't want him to see the panic that pounded in my chest and made my breathing shallow, or my eyebrows hiked up into two question marks.

"Sho, you ain't answering. You heard me?"

"Yes, Daddy."

I thought about my chemistry quiz that I had just bombed at school. It was all about how when an atom's electrons get into their excited states, they may jump from one level to a higher one, or show something different, like a different color. Robert was like that. The blue that gleamed in his eyes was from a new idea that excited him.

"When Daddy talks, you *answer.* Hear me?" He made his voice quiet, but blue flames leaped in his eyes.

"Yes, Daddy." I felt the heat of his breath threaten to melt my frozen face and reveal the cesspool of emotions gurgling within me. *That's why I hate chemistry.* I cleared my throat, choked down the sour stomach that crept up into my mouth, tried to blot my mind of any thoughts. The best I could do was psych myself up for whatever Robert wanted from me.

"Sex is a form of art, Sho. An expressive art. And *I'm* an artist. I need to express myself *inside* of you, not just on top or under you. You need to stop stalling 'cause I'm ready for you, and, you know, you're ready for me too. Your body's callin' me." He sang the last sentence to me—a reference to his 1993 song—and chuckled.

My virginity, that is, my avoidance of the act of sexual intercourse, was the only thing I had managed to keep from Robert. He had tested and measured me, all without penetration. Maybe this was what my English teacher meant when he was trying to explain to my class the other day the meaning of a distinction without a difference and couldn't think of a good example. Maybe I was drawing a line in my mind and calling myself a virgin, a distinction that didn't make a difference. But it made a difference to me. Apparently, it made a difference to Robert, too. I was fifteen now, a sophomore in high school, and Robert said I was ready.

"A man *needs* things from a woman. I'm a sexual man, Sho. You know that. God has given me my musical gifts, my sexual urges, and *you*. He done gave me alla that." He licked his lips. "And Sho, you already know it's mine. I've already had you in a lot of ways. This is how we get closer to each other."

He kissed me. "You see what's around me, Sho. I can have anybody I want. You know that. But I choose *you*. So quit actin' scared now. You've done everything else. I've seen it, touched it, licked it. You don't need to tell me no shit about what you *can't* do. It's what we need. To go higher in our love."

I watched him masturbate casually through his sagged jeans, as his body grew more excited in anticipation of my yes. He penetrated me with his stare. "But if you say no, I'm finna find someone else who'll say *yes*."

I followed his logic. My body had already felt, done, and tasted more things than I wanted to admit, things I was embarrassed by and ashamed of. So why was I holding out? I could see the thought bubble above Robert's head as he licked his lips meaningfully.

I can be replaced. The seed of jealousy that had been planted within me two years before when I knew Aunt Sparkle was giving Robert something he wanted, and that had been watered by the pressure to please him, now sprouted as fear. If I said no, there was another girl, woman, boy, who would say yes. This was how he compelled my yes. But what's a girl's yes to the full size of a grown man?

Robert poured himself into me and I responded. I'm human, after all. But I knew I had lost the last thing I had tried to hold on to. And I knew there would be more dares and new levels. That scared me. With every thrust of him that crushed the breath out of my lungs, I began to understand that Robert's passion was an addiction: his and mine.

After he came, he whispered into the space above my head: "Best remember how I made you feel just now, Sho. How I love to love you."

The weight of his words was heavier than his body on top of me. I shook my head, my braids dragging across his chest.

My basketball team had won the game and we were now in the playoffs! Neither Mom nor Dad would be able to make our first playoff game due to a prior commitment, but when I told Robert I'd be flying solo, he had a different idea. "I can come cheer on my favorite girl!"

"Oh yeah?" Robert's words sounded innocent, but somewhere in my body, I felt like a test or a dare was coming. Something.

"Why you sayin' it like that, Sho? You know I'm a fan of basketball and a fan of you."

I knew. I also knew that whenever Robert came, he stole all the attention. I mean, people came to the games, regardless of whether he was there, of course, but when he came, everybody cranked up the dial on their performance: Both our team and our opponents played harder, the fans cheered louder, the refs were more dramatic, and the spectators gawked at Robert and tried to get pictures with him, no matter what was happening on the court. It was fun to have him sometimes. But this was the playoffs. I didn't want him to distract me or make the refs and our opponents feel like they had to put on a show for him.

"I know." My voice was flat.

Robert raised an eyebrow.

"Daddy," I added.

"Then what's with the face? Is it that you got a boyfriend you don't want me to know about?" He smiled, but his voice had an edge.

"No, Daddy."

"Well, all right, then. 'Sides, you got some cuties up in your school, don't you think?"

I frowned. Girls? Sure, there were plenty of cute girls, and cute boys for that matter. But I wasn't checkin' for any of them like that. I was so consumed with loving Robert that I hadn't given much thought to who else I might like. Robert liked threesomes, though, and I had been intimate with several girls and women of Robert's choosing when the mood struck him. But even though those experiences were designed to produce a sexual response in me, I didn't think I was a lesbian. At least, I thought I preferred boys over girls. But Robert never asked me what I preferred or who I liked. It was always about who *he* liked and what he wanted us to do to each other to please *him*. If we got some pleasure out of it, that was like a bonus.

But girls at school were different. Girls at school were *my* classmates and teammates. I had a relationship with them outside of Robert. So him crushing on them made me nervous.

"You worried, Sho? No need for that. Ain't nobody at that school gonna replace *you*, if that's what you're concerned about. You my best one! You know that."

"But they're my friends, Daddy. And I thought you didn't want anyone to know."

"We not gonna tell just *anyone*. Are we?"

"No, Daddy. Of course not." I felt dizzy.

"Then you find some cuties with tight lips." He snickered. "And maybe we'll have some fun. We'll see. You can just introduce me to some of your girlfriends who could be down. I'll let you know if I agree."

My team lost the game. We were out of the playoffs. But our loss didn't ruin the energy in the gym. We were at the school of the opposing team, and they weren't accustomed to having R. Kelly attend a girls' basketball game. Robert was his regular charming self, smiling for pictures with kids, parents, coaches, and entire families at every time-out for the entire game. I was trying to focus, but it was hard. Squeals of delight broke out at random times, and my teammates seemed as distracted as I was.

After all the hubbub died down following the game, I walked over to Robert with a schoolmate I'll call Brittany. Brittany was about a year older and liked to make scandalous jokes about how she knew R. Kelly had to be a satisfying lover because of the lyrics to his songs. Usually, I just laughed and shook my head to brush off her comments, but this time, I brought her over to Robert to see if he liked her.

She was shy and kept shooting her eyes over at him, unable to look at him directly.

"Girl, you makin' me nervous, now!" Robert chuckled. "Why don't the three of us get a picture!" Robert put his arms around both of our waists while his driver snapped the picture. "Nice meeting you, Brittany! Maybe Reshona can bring you by the studio sometime."

"Okay." Brittany was breathless.

On the next school day, I went on a little fishing expedition. When Brittany and I could speak privately, I worked the conversation around to Robert in the way he had coached me.

"Girl, you lucky! I'm sure I couldn't control myself around R. Kelly. He is just *too* fine!"

"What makes you think I have?" I made a coy smile and waited.

"Wait, what, Shon? What are you telling me right now?!"

"Nothing if you don't lower your damn voice and calm down!"

"Okay, my bad! But what the hell are you saying?" Brittany's voice was an excitable whisper.

"I mean, like you said, he's sexy as all get out. So I do have a little crushy crush!"

Brittany smacked her lips. "Sounds like your crush ain't like my crush. Sounds like you *did* something about it!"

"Maybe I did." I tried to follow Robert's script. Gauge her interest. Tease her but don't give details. See if she can keep secrets.

"Then spill it, Shon!"

"Suppose I tell you something and then I hear it come back to me. Then what?"

"Girl, you know you can trust me! I don't kiss and tell."

"How do I know that?"

"'Cause..." Brittany couldn't think of anything that would be an adequate measure. "Well, have you heard shit about me with anyone?"

"No! Maybe that's because you haven't *been* with anyone!" I shot back.

Brittany looked offended. "Well, I have."

"Mmm." I looked at her pursed lips and arms crossed over her chest. I didn't want to make her mad. Robert had already given me the sign that he liked her, so I couldn't mess things up. "Okay. Tell me the most embarrassing thing you've ever done."

"You mean like fart in public?" Brittany seemed genuinely confused.

"No! Everybody's done that." I rolled my eyes and thought again. I needed to be more specific. "Who's the most embarrassing person you've kissed before?"

Brittany looked sheepish. "Pinky," she whispered. "But that's because this guy I liked said he liked her. But if I kissed her, then he'd kiss me."

"Okay." I nodded and smiled. "Would you kiss me, if you had to?"

"For R. Kelly, I'd do *whatever*." Brittany looked through me. She must have been seeing Robert in her imagination.

"You really got it bad for him!" I laughed.

"Sounds like maybe you do too!"

"Maybe..." Her words brought me back to the job I was supposed to be doing. I played coy again. "Let's talk at the end of the week. If I hear anything about this conversation, I'm gonna tell folks about you and Pinky. But if you know how to keep private stuff private, then maybe you'll get to tell R. Kelly just how much you like him."

"Oh shit, Shon. Really?"

"I'll talk to you Friday, Brittany."

"I'm gonna pee my pants!"

"Don't do that. Just be cute on Friday, okay?"

"Sure! Okay!" Overcome with excitement, Brittany hugged me hard.

I watched her walk away. She was cute in the ways Robert liked: petite with a small waist and a heart-shaped butt and just the right sexy schoolgirl wardrobe to accentuate both. So, since she was his type, she was mine. *Does that make me a lesbian? Or at least bi?* I didn't know. I had kissed girls Robert wanted me to kiss. Sometimes they were blindfolded and naked when I first saw them. I knew how their bodies looked but not their faces, how they kissed but not how they talked. But I knew Brittany's name and face. I knew how she talked and the clothes she liked to wear. She was a real person to me. What would it mean if I kissed her? If I touched her?

Friday came. Brittany could keep secrets. Robert picked us both up from school that day, and I learned what it was like to kiss her. It felt like my submission and Robert's approval. What was it like to touch her? It felt like Brittany's willingness and Robert's pleasure. Brittany's sexual experiences had only been with peers up until that point. I was the knowledgeable one, skilled at teaching less-experienced girls like Brittany what Robert liked while keeping them willing. Brittany wanted to learn whatever I had to teach her.

CHAPTER 4

STAR STUDENT

YOU KNOW HOW A song gets stuck in your head so deep that you can't shake it? Well, given the fact that I was in a situationship with R&B's international hitmaker, I was all too willing to let Robert's every lyric live rent-free in my mind and heart. For me, they were more than just earworms. Robert's sexually charged lyrics were the ultimate playbook, a cheat sheet for his sexual preferences, cravings, and turnoffs. Why was this important? Because I needed Robert to want me most of all. I knew that I wasn't Robert's only girl. He had a wife, for crying out loud, whom the world knew to be my godmother. But even though it seemed to be wrong for him to love me when he had a wife, he said she was okay with his lifestyle. Also, I believed him when he said that our love couldn't play by the world's rules, that it was bigger and stronger than anything he had ever experienced. And since it was for me, too, I just blocked what was wrong about it from my mind and focused on what was right.

Have you ever wanted something so bad that you're willing to do whatever you need to get it? And when you feel like it can be snatched from you at any moment, you can feel like you want it even more. To the core of my being, I felt myself to be who Robert said I was and worth the price he put on me. As he explained it, his love for me made him willing to lie for me, to jeopardize his entire home life and career for me. He made sure I always knew just how high the stakes were for him. And I believed them to be equally high for me. The only thing that I felt as much as my love for Robert was my jealousy toward all the other females who were a part of his world sexually. I didn't really differentiate between the women who were eighteen and above and those who were underage like me. I couldn't. Because if I did, I'd have had to go down the rabbit hole of *Well, what about you, Reshona? Why are you in a full-on sexual relationship with a grown man?* Despite all the grown-up activity that had become my day-to-day, I lacked the mental bandwidth to have that conversation with myself.

Here's the thing about being exposed to sex and sexual manipulation as a young teenager. It opens you up to a world that you're not mentally capable of understanding. My child's mind didn't know that the way my body responded to what Robert did to it was straight biology and that he didn't have some sort of magical power over me. It felt like he did, like he alone could make my body feel sexy.

You might clutch your pearls at the thought of a girl of thirteen, fourteen, or fifteen wanting to be sexy to *anyone*, much less a grown man. But while there are teen girls who are only thinking about their next game of double Dutch or catching their favorite Disney TV show, lots are learning what the culture says it means to be a woman in training. Teen girls wonder whether people see them as attractive, how to be more desirable, and if they'll ever have a boyfriend (or girlfriend). They want to be a part of the pretty girls' club. Why? Because most of the fashion, music, and popular culture teach girls to be eye candy that boys and men won't be able to resist.

For me, I was trying to grow into all these new feelings and expectations, and wrestling with my previous identity as a tomgirl, all while receiving oral sex from a grown-ass man who the world called my godfather.

I didn't have any idea what it meant to be groomed by an older and more experienced person and that Robert was manipulating me to do and be what he wanted. I couldn't understand that when Robert explained things to me, he used my youth and naivete to gaslight me and make me question everything my parents had ever taught me about honesty or doing the right thing. I didn't know that love bombing was one of the strategies Robert used regularly to make me feel closer to him and indebted to him at the same time. While I was living in the emotional chaos that I believed to be love and devotion to Robert, I couldn't have any perspective on the reality of what was going on. I was just so needy for his possessive and oppressive brand of love that I wanted him to want me the *most.* I needed him to love me the *best.* And I practiced being the girl he wanted.

Robert was an exacting teacher. He knew how far to push me to keep me off-balance and on a constant quest to fulfill his growing list of expectations. He taught me that jealousy, fear, and especially obedience were his love languages.

"People do shit they don't want to for the folks they love every damn day of the week, Sho. Know that!"

"Yes, Daddy."

I was an excellent student. Under Robert's tutelage, I became expert at lying to my parents. He trained me on what to say, how to say it, what my body language should be if ever they pushed back on my desire to spend time with my godfamily. Maybe it was my perfect performances that kept any growing concerns from my parents at bay. Or maybe it all looked good from their perspective. It was hard to say…

With Robert, there always seemed to be an expiration date on his tests, no matter how high my grade. I was only as good as my latest exercise of submission, and loyalty and blind obedience were the only love currency Robert would accept from me.

Whenever I questioned his requests or even hesitated to comply, Robert had a form of correction that he knew would get me back in line. Sometimes I had to watch another person come and pleasure him in the way he had wanted me to. It was horrible to be forced to watch someone else's naked body do what I refused to. When they came in, they were often blindfolded so they couldn't see me. I was his secret, and he didn't want someone to be able to identify me. Sometimes, after I watched, he would force me to join and have me perform a sex act with the blindfolded person as a test. It always felt like a test that I had better pass the first time.

Despite the fact that I was his best girl, who tried to follow his every instruction and who always wanted his approval even when I was uncomfortable, there was always a steady stream of new tests. I didn't know how many others there were in addition to his wife, Andrea. But he had a way of making you want to strive to be top of the class in obeying and pleasing him. After I brought in Brittany and then Pinky, too, to engage in threesomes with Robert, he started to have sex with them without me. In the twisted logic I was operating under, their secret meetings with Robert felt like they had betrayed me. I stopped being friends with them because of it.

I remember times when I did act uncomfortable about performing the perverted sex acts Robert wanted from me. Even going back to when he was sleeping with Aunt Sparkle and there were plenty of things I still hadn't done, like sexual intercourse, Robert would act wounded, and his energy would shift if I hesitated.

"Don't worry about it, Sho. You don't have to do it," Robert said, his voice flat and shoulders sagging.

I sat there, feeling bad because Robert felt bad. Then, because I couldn't figure out what else to do, I started biting my nails. Robert began rummaging through some of his videotapes.

"Look at this, Sho."

I sat silently as the exposed privates of Robert and a woman I couldn't identify came to life in front of me. Robert liked tight camera angles, so I squinted my eyes until they were nearly slits to block the graphic sights and sounds that loomed large on the TV screen. Seeing movement on the couch, I shot my eyes over to Robert. His hand was down his pants.

Robert heaved and stopped the tape. "That's what I'm talking about, Sho! *That's* how I want you to be for Daddy."

I had no words.

"If she can do me like that and I don't give a shit about her, I know you'd blow my mind, baby. Can't you do that for Daddy?"

I watched Robert's eyes scan my face. He pulled his lips into a tight line in a look of disapproval. "I can't believe you gonna let other women bust my nuts while you just sit there."

I sat there, scared. I knew I was supposed to say yes, but judging from the sounds made by the woman on the videotape and what I saw, what Robert wanted was going to hurt.

"All right then." Robert pulled his lips tighter. "I thought you loved me enough, Sho. But maybe *I'm* the fool. Maybe I'm just some nigga you messin' with. That's fucked up, Sho." Nodding at his own statement, he slid to the other end of the couch where we both sat, and dialed his cell phone. He put the call on speakerphone as soon as someone answered. I couldn't place her voice. Giving directions to the voice on the line, Robert's tone was playful but commanding, and his expectations were clear. He hung up and threw his phone down. It almost hit me. "*This* is why you shouldn't tell Daddy no."

I started biting the skin around my pointer finger and thumb because the nails were already gone. I knew she would be in soon. She was probably in the vocal booth, and Robert instructed her to get ready in the closet at the back of that room. A door at the back of the closet led to the little room we were in. Robert was rolling his neck and loosening his shoulders to get ready for her arrival.

Three minutes later, someone knocked on the door between the vocal booth closet and the secret room where we were. Robert got up, his jeans now sagging below his naked behind, and walked to the door. He tied a blindfold on a young woman before she could see me in the dim light of our windowless box of a room. She had on a bra but no panties, and her hair was pulled into two hasty pigtails. Robert guided her to the couch and positioned her.

As I sat not three feet from them, I felt queasy and anxious. Robert seemed fixated on all that was happening with the blindfolded girl. It was clear that I had been dismissed.

When the action finally slowed, Robert turned his face toward me. "You see what *she* does for me!" He slung his words at me over the sounds of her groans, his breath as hot and funky as the thick air around us.

Jealousy, insecurity, and fear were a toxic soup that soaked through me and short-circuited my brain. That's how I learned that, even if I wanted to say no, it felt safer for my mental health to go along with his program and say yes.

It's wild how your abuser can compel your yes and then make you believe it was your choice. And it tears down your sense of self because you start to believe that their fetishes are yours since you're the one performing those vile actions. It's a mindfuck. My adult self had to learn to release all those lies and the shame that came with them. I did *not* want what Robert wanted. He was always playing the long game with me. Forcing me to execute on his short-term steps was designed to get me to his goal of my being completely submissive to his will and dependent on him for every aspect of who I was. That kind of dependency breeds unwavering loyalty, even if you feel like shit doing it.

For as much as I thought myself to be a welcome presence at Robert's studio because I was his goddaughter, I was still very much out of my element in the space. Full of adult language, activities, and preoccupations, the studio housed as many eyes and ears as it did secrets. I was too young and too preoccupied with keeping track of the lies that filled my mouth to notice. My words and actions were for an audience of one. If Robert seemed pleased that I had managed to say the right things to his celebrity visitors and say very little to everyone else, then Robert was the only person to whom I could voice my relief, in private. If I messed up, Robert's manipulative and biting words crushed my spirit and kept me needy for his approval.

Though there were many folks on payroll at the Chocolate Factory, Robert's studio, I didn't know who was paying enough attention to me to suss out what was going on. Their poker faces kept me ignorant. But folks knew when I was around. And Aunt Sparkle, who no longer had any business at Robert's studio, still had some of her people who were her eyes and ears there and would answer her questions. Apparently, many of her questions were about me.

Aunt Sparkle came to know that I was spending lots of time at the studio, sometimes without my dad being there at all. As a young woman navigating the messy R&B music business and who had once been Robert's protégée (in addition to being one of his lovers), Aunt Sparkle had spent many hours in the rooms of many studios and knew something about what could happen during all those unsupervised hours.

She wasn't wrong.

I don't know who my dad was talking to at Robert's studio, if anyone, what he saw, or if he knew about the world that Aunt Sparkle had introduced me to. In one of our conversations before he passed away in 2021, Dad explained to me that he was naive, willfully ignorant of the possibilities of what could have been going on because the reality—that he had a steady paycheck as a session guitarist for Robert and that I seemed to be happy—drowned out everything else. As a man who had spent decades carving out a living in support of his family by working in studios and on stages with Christian and secular artists alike, my dad had learned not to believe everything he heard. Gossip stuck to the walls like glue in the music industry, but he chose to keep his head above the fray (and sometimes stuck in the sand) rather than be dragged into the swirl of messiness. Dad knew that lies circulated quicker than the truth and most of it wasn't his business anyway, so he played his guitar and then left.

As far as Dad was concerned, our family's association with Robert Kelly was a net positive. Dad had a gig, Sparkle had an album, and I had a godfather. Dad didn't know as much as I did about what had made Aunt Sparkle's business relationship with Robert explode. She didn't tell him and he knew better than to ask. Sure, Dad like the rest of Chicago (and the world) had heard the rumor that Robert married his artist Aaliyah when she was fifteen, but again, he didn't think it had legs, so he didn't put any stock in it. What Dad had witnessed firsthand was that Robert had given his life to Christ and committed to being a better man. Sure, Robert's music was suggestive, but plenty of performing artists had a persona that differed from who they really were. So, Dad explained, most times he paid little attention to the whispers in the peanut gallery.

My teenage self didn't know most of this, but at the time I was happy for Dad's willful ignorance. There was one instance, however, when Dad traded in that ignorance for a moment of discernment.

My family was sitting in our living room having our regular weekly Bible study. I was curled up on our cozy navy-blue sofa with lil Greg snuggled up beside me. Mom was his bookend, and we all sat across from Dad. I had just finished reading aloud the scripture Dad told me to, and he was going over the lesson in the Bible. His voice was so forceful that I straightened my back and put my feet on the floor. My mind could barely think about what he was saying, just that he said it with so much conviction. Then Dad snapped his Bible shut and told us to bow our heads in a posture of submission to God. Dad started, his voice dipped in the blood of the Lamb.

"Father God, we come against every spirit of perversion and deception that is claiming this modern age. By the power of the Holy Spirit, I *rebuke* them in the name of Jesus!"

My head bowed, I shuddered under the weight of my dad's prayer. I bowed lower.

"We rebuke the hand of the enemy on our son and *especially* our daughter, Lord. We lay every sin of sexual immorality, of coveting, and of lying at your feet, dear Jesus!"

Dad's words injected fear into my very soul. I felt my spirit wrestling inside of me.

With Bible study and my father's prayer done, I hurriedly excused myself from the room. I felt naked, like Dad told me all about myself; with his words, he tore off every lie I had rehearsed and repeated to them. I couldn't bear to have any of them look at me and see me stripped of all my lies about the true nature of my relationship with Robert.

For as exposed as I felt by your prayer that day, Dad, I wish that version of you, full of holy boldness and speaking truth to power, would have shown up like that more often.

I wish you had taken up more space and crowded out Robert's authority over me, asserting that our family's rules still applied to me, even when I was in his space.

I wish you had insisted that you enter Robert's environment, meet his wife and child, and see where I would sleep during sleepovers.

I wish your intuition had kicked in when I seemed uncomfortable and would refuse to speak to or even acknowledge any man who was not you or Robert.

I wish you had been suspicious enough to catch Robert in the act of making sneaky sexual gestures toward me while I fidgeted, unable to respond and afraid someone might see.

I wish you had noticed the confusion that lurked behind my smiles, the distress that creased my forehead, and my uncharacteristic silence.

Dad, I never doubted your love for me. I just wish that your love could have pushed past your fear and *fought* for me.

* * *

Two weeks later, my parents and I had another come-to-Jesus meeting.

The knock on my bedroom door was insistent. "Come in here. Now." Dad's voice had more bass in it than usual. He hadn't asked me to come; he *told* me.

I hurried off the phone and went to the living room.

"Where's lil Greg?" I wondered. It was practically dinnertime. Why wasn't he home?

"He's spending the night with Granny," Mom answered from where she rocked herself on the sofa. Her voice was raw and her face puffy from recently cried tears.

I looked at Dad. His face was stamped with anger. He perched at the edge of his favorite chair. I pushed myself into the far corner of the blue sofa to get as far away from Mom and Dad as possible.

Dad sighed. "Your Aunt Stephanie has been in touch with the Illinois Department of Children and Family Services, Reshona. They've launched an investigation. Seems she thinks you may be involved in some indecent sexual activity at Robert's studio and that it's with Robert. What do you have to say about that, Reshona?"

My mouth hung open in shock. Luckily, my mother muttered something into the dead air.

"I can't believe she'd call DCFS on us! That's not how we handle things. Why is she taking her problems out on us?"

"Valerie, Reshona hasn't answered."

They both looked at me.

"That's crazy!" I wrestled my real emotions into something that looked like anger. "How dare she do that?" I looked from Mom to Dad. Finding a more receptive expression from my mother, I turned back to her. "I mean, he's my godfather. She's the one who suggested it. I know she's mad that things broke bad with them. I mean, with her business with him. But he's still my godfather!" I let my tears fall freely.

"So, you're telling us that none of that is true?" Dad twitched from the effort of looking at me through his discomfort. Mom was wringing her hands.

"Of course not!" Latching on to Aunt Sparkle's indiscretion again, I turned back to my mom. "Why would Aunt Sparkle say that? Why would she call DCFS? That's crazy."

Dad didn't answer my question because he couldn't. "I'm talking to you like this, Reshona, because I want you to remember that you weren't raised that way. There is no blessing in cheating with another woman's husband."

"I'm not *cheating* on anybody! They're my godparents! Robert and Andrea. I play with their kid. What's the problem with that? I can't say the same for Aunt Sparkle, but I'm not doing anything wrong!" I worked myself into a nearly hysterical anger, parroting all the lies Robert had drummed into my head, without missing a beat.

"We've never been intimate."

"We've never even been alone together, so there's never been an opportunity for something like that."

"Andrea is my godmother, and their daughter is like my own sister. My love and loyalty lie with them."

As Robert had instructed me, I weaved the few threads of truth into the dense fabric of lies seamlessly. And because he had rehearsed me so many times, I knew how to coordinate my facial expressions and body language with my words so that I could convincingly deflect their every suspicion.

"That damn Stephanie! She's gonna mess around and have our children taken from us."

"Valerie, nobody's taking anybody."

"That's what happens when the law gets all mixed up in family concerns. Especially Black families. Stephanie knows that!" Righteous anger rolled off my mother in waves.

"Is this conversation over?" I borrowed Mom's righteous indignation.

"For now." Dad's voice had been reduced to a whisper.

I stormed out of the living room and marched straight to my bedroom, resisting the urge to slam my door since that was Mom's pet peeve. I couldn't afford to make her angry with me since she was my biggest ally. Then I grabbed my phone, crawled into the bottom of my closet, and called Robert. Who else was I going to run to?

My parents were distraught. Dad's deflated posture and Mom's tears made it clear to me just how much it crushed them to imagine the possibility that their fifteen-year-old daughter could be sexually entangled with Robert. We had finished our first conversation, but Mom and Dad had more questions. With fresh lies in my mouth, I was emphatic in my denials and distressed that they could even entertain any accusation of Robert hurting me.

"Dad, don't you remember when you were feeling so stressed out because Grandpa Bo was sick and Robert gave us the gift of a nice dinner at that restaurant you wanted to try?"

"Of course." Dad nodded, the memory dampening his eyes with tears. "It was just what the doctor ordered."

"Exactly. That's who Robert is to us. He's thoughtful. He thinks of our family as his own." I turned and looked at Mom.

"How can you all of a sudden call him a monster! How can you accept his kindness and all the ways he's tried to create nice experiences for us, and then accuse him of something Aunt Sparkle made up?"

Mom's face was crisscrossed with sorrow. "That's not what we're doing, Reshona."

"Then what *are* you doing?" I made my face look more pained than hers.

"We had to *ask*, Reshona. You're our daughter and these are serious accusations. Even if they are from Stephanie. We can't just *ignore* them!" Not wanting even one word of what she heard from Aunt Sparkle to be true, Mom sounded like she was trying to convince herself.

"Well, I answered you. Okay?" I glanced at Dad's face again. He looked conflicted. I couldn't stand to look at him. "Can I go to my room?"

Mom waved her hand.

My parents didn't say anything else to me. They *wanted* to believe me, to believe the words Robert had given me. Robert wanted my parents to feel a sense of guilt and indebtedness for even doubting him, and they did. As quickly as these allegations intruded into our lives, my parents wrapped their arms tightly around our family of four and faced them down, complete with our ironclad agreement about all the necessary alibis. I was relieved.

Robert was proud of me; I had passed my most difficult loyalty test to date. I had stood up for our love. And now Mom, Dad, Robert, and I all had Aunt Sparkle in our cross hairs.

My parents had an obvious interest in proving these allegations to be false. At fifteen, I wasn't focused on this aspect of things beyond what they said, that Sparkle's reckless allegations could rip both me and my little brother away from my parents and land us in the foster care system. When I talked to Robert, he put flesh on the bones of his dire concerns. If the allegations were substantiated enough to result in charges against *him*, he could lose his career and family and end up in jail. I didn't want either thing to happen. I was clear that my convincing lies were the only things that stood in the way of my entire life falling down around me.

Less clear at the time—but surely clear to both my parents and Robert—was the fact that the adults around me could be severely punished if the DCFS investigation amounted to anything. Of course, Robert could be found guilty of sexual abuse of a minor. But if folks in Robert's orbit or outside of it—Aunt Sparkle included—testified in family court that my dad would leave me at the studio without him, he could have a lot of explaining to do. And if it came out that my parents dropped me off for sleepovers at Robert's house when they had never even seen the inside of his house or met my godmother, Andrea, no one would have cared that they were trying to respect how protective Robert was of his wife, daughter, and their personal space. Mom and Dad could have been found guilty of child neglect. As an adult and a mother myself, I now understand how scary these allegations must have been for them. They loved my brother and me, no doubt. But now a cloud hung over their parenting of me and the custody they had of both their children was in jeopardy.

Unfortunately, my parents were still far from allowing themselves to believe that the love Robert showed our family, up to and including my dad's job as his musician, had been him grooming *them* to trust him and see only the best in him. They were in defense mode, which made it impossible for them to consider that they might have been duped. For reasons I didn't then know, it was easier for them to feel betrayed by Aunt Sparkle than suckered by Robert. After all, she was the one who had chosen to air our alleged dirty laundry and jeopardize our family unit in the process.

I thought this was what had driven a wedge between Aunt Sparkle and my mother. But they had chosen sides about Robert well before DCFS got involved. It would be decades before I learned that Mom knew a bit about Aunt Sparkle and Robert's sexual intimacy through their sister-talk, and that Aunt Sparkle had explained that Robert kicked her off his record label after her hush-hush situation with her boyfriend blew up. Once she was ousted, Aunt Sparkle believed, her whole family should have stepped right along with her. She felt that having me still galivanting around the studio as his goddaughter while my dad continued as one of his musicians was a betrayal of our blood relationship with her.

Mom didn't see it that way. Sure, Robert was messy, and he did Aunt Sparkle dirty, but what had Aunt Sparkle thought would happen? She had to have known that when sexual and professional relationships get intertwined, pulling them back apart is usually a hot garbage mess. So as far as Mom was concerned, Aunt Sparkle was wrong to expect her family to break ranks with Robert because her illicit entanglement with him went south.

That initial dispute between Mom and Aunt Sparkle the year before set the stage for this next showdown between them. Already suspicious of Aunt Sparkle, Mom now smelled a rat. How could it be that Robert was a blessing to our family when Aunt Sparkle's career was flourishing, but now that they were on the outs, all of a sudden he was molesting *me*? The timing of Aunt Sparkle's about-face struck Mom as a little too coincidental.

Dad agreed that Aunt Sparkle was an unreliable messenger, so he was equally skeptical. He also knew that for as much as Aunt Sparkle didn't like folks messing with *her* money, she seemed willing to mess with Dad's, a point that left a sour taste in his mouth. And because he usually walked in the opposite direction of confrontation, I think he found it easier to agree with Mom and join in her frustration with her sister rather than think the worst of Robert and have to confront what it meant that his boss—who acted like he liked him—might have been exploiting his daughter right under his nose.

My dazed and confused self had already parted ways with the truth, so I latched on to my parents' distrust of Aunt Sparkle's intentions. Then Robert explained it was better for me—for *us*—if my parents directed their anger at Aunt Sparkle for her lack of concern for our family.

He underscored his point with his own dose of Sparkle bashing. "Look, Sho, I know you love your aunt and all, but she's an angry woman who wants payback from *me*. Unlucky for you, she don't mind throwing you under the bus for it!"

"Under the bus?" I was already upset and now Robert was scaring me.

"She don't mind if you suffer because of our beef, because she got a beef with me."

My understanding came with a punch to the gut.

"I'm sorry, Sho. Betrayal is a mofo. Ask me how I know."

Mom and I sat at the kitchen table when she said the same thing in her own way. Her tone was more measured but no less direct. "Reshona, I'm afraid your Aunt Stephanie just wasn't thinking about how much trouble she could create for us all. Her career's been struggling ever since her first album came out, so she's scared and worried. I get that. But if she's trying to make herself feel better about things, this is *not* the way to do it." Mom patted my arm.

I didn't know how to feel. *Was* she jealous of me? I knew she had stirred up feelings of jealousy and competition in me a couple of years before I could name what those feelings were. I knew she once was sleeping with Robert and now I was. I knew I had spilled the secret about her boyfriend when she warned me not to and that her worst fears came true. Maybe she *was* angry at me, willing to let my suffering be collateral damage for what she felt Robert had done to her.

The truth was more complex than what my fifteen-year-old self could comprehend. All I knew was that since Aunt Sparkle didn't care enough about me and my family to protect us, her concerns were bogus at best.

Sometimes you're not the target.

Sometimes your weak spots are in their blind spots.

Sometimes your pain triggers theirs.

Sometimes their anger is deflection.

PART TWO

BAG LADY

One day all them bags gon' get in your way.

—Erykah Badu

CHAPTER 5

THE DEVIL IN THE DETAILS

IN ADDITION TO THE Ten Commandments, my family had eight more. Kids were to:

11. Fear God (that is, be scared of him).
12. Respect your elders—including parents, older relatives, teachers, and folks at church—even if you don't agree with everything they say.
13. Not suck your teeth or roll your eyes at an adult (or you might get slapped).
14. Say grace before meals, even when eating out.
15. Say your prayers at night, because you could die before you wake up.
16. Eat *everything* on your dinner plate because there are kids starving in other countries.
17. Say please and thank you.
18. Not get into grown folks' business.

With our eighteen commandments chiseled into our minds and the blood of Jesus purifying our hearts, my churchgoing family was saved and sanctified. *All* of us were: my cousins, aunts, and uncles included. I must have been six or seven years old when I first heard one of my older relatives mention the great cloud of witnesses. As an adult, I now know that phrase comes from Hebrews 12:1, which talks about all the godly folks who came before us and are now cheering us on from heaven as we try to live godly lives ourselves. But when I was a kid, I was sure the cloud of witnesses was made up of my family's holy rollers here on earth, especially Dad's parents—pastor and first lady of the church we attended—and Mom's father, who was a deacon there. It was through my super-saved family elders that I learned the importance of choosing God's path to salvation—the narrow gate—instead of the wide gate that led to everything bad and sinful.

For years, I couldn't for the life of me figure out why God would make the path to him so narrow. And even though I knew that God liked to forgive us our sins, I wasn't sure that he'd keep forgiving *me* if I committed the same sins over and over again. I wish I could have asked Grandpa Bo about this or even checked in with Mom or Dad to see if they knew, but I didn't have the courage to ask. Yes, courage. As simple as my questions seem, and as easy as it would have been to get my answers, the truth is that I didn't grow up questioning adults about the things they said. Adults were to be respected and believed. Their rules were to be followed (see commandments twelve, thirteen, and eighteen). And since I already knew that God was supposed to be obeyed and I kept slipping up in that department, if a respected adult said something about God, every instinct inside of me made me fear God and shame myself into silence for the added sin of questioning God's instruction spoken through an authority figure.

By the time I was about fifteen, I was clear I was a sinner with a capital *S*. But my understanding of faith, forgiveness, free choice, and my family's picture-perfect holiness wasn't. Further complicating all of that was a poem I had recently studied in school: Robert Frost's "The Road Not Taken." It seemed that the road that wasn't taken was the better road but, for some reason, the writer had chosen the one that was worse. Why did he choose the wrong road? How long did it take before he realized he had chosen poorly? And had he chosen the wrong road because it was wide?

I wondered all these things about myself as much as I did about the poet. But even though I wanted to ask my teacher, I felt too embarrassed to ask in front of my classmates. And I feared that asking my parents would make them suspicious about why I was asking. So instead, I quietly wrestled with the road I had chosen that led me to my relationship with Robert and the wide gate and broad road of lies, deception, and confusion that became my life. What if I had chosen the other road? Would I be sad like the poet? Would I have missed not having a secret sexual relationship with Robert? Or would my life have been better?

What made this all the more perplexing was that the road I was on—wide and sin-filled as it was—felt narrow and constricting. I second-guessed every feeling I had or idea I thought. *Everything* I said and did had to be approved by Robert. That is, everything except for my participation in my group, 4 The Cause. Sure, it was stressful having to hold in so many lies about my life. I could hardly talk to my cousins about normal teen stuff, or anything at all really. I was always afraid they'd ask me if I had a boyfriend or liked someone, and I'd have to tell another convincing lie. The more lies I told, the more I had to keep track of, because if I didn't, I might get caught in a lie later and life could start to blow up in my face. And it certainly didn't help that Robert would guilt-trip me whenever I was away from him for more than a couple of days. But 4 The Cause was *mine*. It was the only thing I did in my life that had nothing to do with Robert.

My phone rang four times before I picked up.

"Did you speak to your parents about what we discussed yesterday?" Robert didn't bother to say hello or make small talk.

"No, Daddy." My voice eked out of me. I was afraid he might yell at me. He didn't. I pulled my bed's covers over top of me like a tent.

"Listen, Sho, I been thinkin' heavy about us. About our love, you know. This shit right here is so special, we gotta *protect* it. Even if we gotta do things we wouldn't normally do." His voice cracking on the last syllable, he paused and sniffled into the phone.

I imagined he was crying. I was, too. My body pulled into a ball under my covers; I became hot. I kicked my covers off and looked around my room. The tears in my eyes made all my shiny basketball trophies and school plaques look like a blurry kaleidoscope of colors. My fast breathing was amplified by the phone. I couldn't trust myself to answer, so I didn't. I knew where this conversation was heading.

"Baby, I know you sad, but think about me, about *us*. We *gotta* keep things quiet around you so nobody starts trippin' you up, or me either, with all them photographers taking high-quality pictures of you out on tour with that group."

He said "that group" like the name of my group was a curse word he wouldn't force himself to say. I sighed into the phone.

"Sho!"

"Yes, Daddy."

"I need you to hear me good." He paused long enough to oblige me to listen with my whole body. "At this point, that group you in is a liability. I mean, it's time for you to cut out as many wild cards as you can and simplify your life. We don't need niggas trying to charm their dicks inside you when I ain't around. We just need you to fly under the radar, you know. You can't do that if you rappin' centerstage at some concert in Germany or some shit. I know what these men want from you, Sho. How can I *protect* you? All I wanna do is protect you, baby."

My tears were flowing faster than I could wipe them. "It's just—"

"I know it's hard, Sho." Robert cut me off. "I get it. But, as an artist, you know, you gotta make tough decisions sometimes. Cut your losses when shit ain't right for you no more."

"But I *like* rapping with my cousins! I *like* touring with the group!"

"See, you comin' with that 'I like' shit again? Damn, Sho! Look, real artists do shit they don't like all the time. What's that group getting you now? Sure, you've toured around Europe a bit, and you had some fun for a while, but what else? Don't nobody even *know* you in America. I mean, not for your rapping with that group. I bet you met more stars hangin' around *my* studio than you ever met as a Black girl rapper in fucking Italy. And if you want the latest Jordans or whatever, you ain't gotta rap for them or even ask your parents. You know Daddy will get them shits for you! So what's the point in jumping on a plane to rap for folks who don't understand a damn thing you're sayin'? Besides, I bet it costs y'all more money than you make to go on tour in Europe, and that don't even make sense." He snickered.

I couldn't figure out how to respond to any of Robert's claims, so I said nothing. For all I knew, he was right. After all, 4 The Cause wasn't being called for gigs like we were when I was little. I was still short, but I wasn't a novelty like I was when I was spitting bars out of my ten-year-old mouth. I started biting at the corner of my pointer finger until it bled. Then I bit down on it to make it stop. I looked around my bedroom at the yellowing music posters on my walls, the janky cassette recorder that had been my parents' thirteenth birthday gift to me, and my Sony Discman, brand-new Avirex jacket, and limited edition Jordans still sitting in a heap in the middle of my floor where I had dropped them.

I stared at my pile of CDs from every artist who had come to Robert's Chicago Trax studio, and thought about the smile plastered on my face when Robert surprised me and I walked into the vocal booth only to find Usher, my celebrity crush. My eyes bounced over to the photos sticking in the corner of my mirror of me cheesing with Trin-i-tee 5:7, the Isley Brothers, Syleena Johnson, Ja Rule, and Jay-Z. My mind somersaulted through all the times I had received VIP treatment in Chi-town. It was never because I was the pint-sized rapper in 4 The Cause and *always* because I was Robert's goddaughter. And I thought about the overwhelming and sometimes scary love that Robert poured into my body and fed to my mind with his silver tongue and knowledgeable hands. All the nicest things I ever owned were gifts from Robert. All my best experiences in recent memory were supplied through Robert.

It was as if Robert had upgraded my former life and every path led to him.

This is what they want you to think—the person who controls you, berates you, calls out your name, and makes you feel insecure. They want you to believe that every road to your dreams leads to them. They won't let you be great, and then they gaslight you into thinking it's because there's no greatness in you. Sometimes they use their money, fame, and influence to make you small in your own eyes. They keep reminding you that you can't afford the lifestyle they can provide you with, and they convince you that you *never* will.

Sometimes the gifts are smaller: the wig, the bag, the piercings, the concert tickets. Or maybe it's the clothing they require you to wear or the food they get for you to eat.

But stuff isn't the only way they get into your head. It's the snide looks that say you're trash, that you're unworthy. The words thrown at you like an ax to your heart. The love withheld. The dreams shut down. The opportunities they make you give up. Sometimes it's forcing you to have a baby...or not to have one. Or to forgo your education, bury your talent, second-guess your own intuition.

Maybe you don't recognize your own abuse because you think it can only look like a slap across the face, or that rape only happens between strangers on a dark road. Perhaps you think the schoolyard is where bullying occurs. So you don't see how you've been exploited. You may have learned that *love* is a word that makes you obligated to comply and be grateful. But love's an action. It's patience and kindness, not envy or boastfulness. Love doesn't dishonor you, belittle you, or try to keep you stuck and make you beg.

When they tell you that they make your life better, ask yourself: Do they bring pain or comfort to your body, encouragement or stress to your mind, and peace or turmoil to your spirit? Don't take their word for it, either. Remember, your peace of mind is worth more than any material gift someone might dangle in front of you. And love doesn't come with strings attached. Give yourself permission to love who you are right now, even if you don't have all you want and haven't realized all your dreams. You're still enough. Just by being here, you offer the world a light that no one else can shine.

Returning my mind to the conversation, I could imagine Robert's self-satisfied smile.

"Right, baby. Now you're understanding me. You don't need one more thing from that group. Not no more. It done ran its course,

Sho. And every day you're on the road is another day you can slip up and say some shit we both gonna regret. Besides, when you're gone, I miss you, baby. You my *best* one."

Robert licked his lips loudly through the phone. I frowned, but he couldn't hear that.

"I can just about taste you right now, Sho." He licked them again. "What's more important than our love?"

I felt a shiver run through me despite myself. "It's not more important—"

"Then why are we still having this conversation, Sho?"

The silence over the phone line was oppressive.

"Look, I got people in the vocal booth waiting for me to get back to it, you know. I'm sorry, but I can't keep sitting here listening to you breathe when you know like I do what needs to happen."

"Okay."

"Okay, *what*?"

"Okay, Daddy?"

"Man, shit! That's all you got? Has this goddamn conversation been a waste of my goddamn time, Sho?" Robert's voice was a hiss.

"No, Daddy! It's just—"

"Look! Have I ever steered you wrong? I fucking love the shit outta you! You my best girl. Why I even gotta say that?" His voice cracked again. He sighed. In my mind's eye, I could see his shoulders slumping, the heaviness of his words weighing him down. "Check it, Sho. I know this fucking sucks right now. But *we're* worth it, baby. And I believe in you." He sent a loud kiss through the phone. "Will you tell your parents you're leaving the group?"

"Yes, Daddy."

"Okay, now! And whatchu gonna tell them?"

"That... that I don't want to keep traveling and missing school.

That I wanna be a regular teenager and that the group feels like a waste of time."

"*That's* what I'm about, Sho!" I could hear him smiling. "You a diamond, baby. Look, I gotta jet. But remember, I'm sending you all kinds of love and strength and everything. I'm as close to you as your mind. Know that."

"Yes, Daddy."

I got off the phone feeling drained. I knew what to say to my parents. But wouldn't my explanation raise eyebrows?

I didn't do it that night. I couldn't. I was afraid I would cry, that the words in my mind wouldn't come out of my mouth right. Robert didn't take the news of my delayed conversation well. While our first few conversations had been mostly encouraging and full of reminders of how important our love was, the following pep talk was full of expressions of disappointment and implied threats. I knew I couldn't go another day without doing what he told me to, and risk physical discipline to go with his verbal reprimands that cut down to the bone. The trauma of that conversation—of fearing my parents' reaction on the one hand and Robert's wrath on the other—has made it hard for me to remember some of the specifics of it even now. What I do remember is my queasy stomach full of intimidation as I looked for a way to sit them down and convince them that I no longer wanted the one thing in my life that was still mine and not Robert's. Ironically, I feared that my decision would somehow shine a spotlight on my situation with Robert, because maybe they'd realize it was his words coming out of my mouth.

The conversation was awkward because the lies rang so loudly in my own head. *I miss going to school dances and hanging with my friends.*

I want a normal social life. I watched my parents' faces twitch from the pain of my words. They were taking it in, *believing* me. They agreed with some of my points and accepted my decision. They took the tears in my eyes as tears of relief. But I was grieving.

Telling my cousins why I didn't want to perform with them anymore was as difficult as telling my parents. I could see the hurt on their faces. My words implicated them; my rationale sounded like they weren't worth my time anymore, and made everyone question what the "cause" was and why *any* of us were ever committed to it. Needless to say, the morale of the group and my relationship with my cousins both took a hit. For the remaining year or two that 4 The Cause continued to exist, the group filled my old spot with another cousin who favored me in terms of her physique and rapping ability. But unfortunately for her, when the shit hit the fan with the videotape of Robert and me a couple of years later, some of the internet bullying intended for me ended up being directed at my cousin. Every now and again, she *still* sometimes gets hate messages meant for me.

Robert had lots of rules and following them took lots of energy. Because our relationship was supposed to be a secret—although by 1999 many members of his staff knew, though they've sworn ignorance—I would have to switch up at any time of day or night and act the part of Robert's goddaughter that he wanted me to play. His five biggest rules were:

1. Don't make eye contact with any man.
2. No talking to men other than my dad or grandpa without Robert there.

3. No calling Robert "Daddy" in front of people.
4. Be pleasant but not chatty so my interest won't make someone think I'm flirting.
5. Don't wear clothing that shows my cleavage or shape, and wear platform shoes to appear taller and older.

The mental prep that it took to be so many different versions of myself was exhausting because, sometimes, I had no idea who Robert wanted me to be. If I messed up—by talking too much or too little, acting too interested or too bored—Robert might punish me, so sometimes I would just try to avoid people or pretend to be sleepy so I didn't have to speak too much.

Once when I was in the common room backstage at one of Robert's concerts, there were a bunch of friends, family, and staff standing around, and a long table loaded with lots of sandwiches, drinks, and other refreshments. George Daniels called out to me.

I dropped my head and acted as if I couldn't hear him.

"Shon, didn't you hear me?" He spoke louder and stooped down to my level.

Of course I heard him. Of course I knew him. George Daniels was legendary in the Chicago music scene, the godfather of Chicago music who was responsible for launching so many music careers. His West Side store, George's Music Room, was a required stop for any Black artist promoting their latest album and a place I grew up visiting with Dad. But now I was seeing George Daniels at Robert's concert in my role as Robert's goddaughter. Without Robert to referee the conversation, I knew I couldn't talk to him. No exceptions. Afraid of breaking Robert's rule, I whipped my whole body around and started talking to a woman on staff with Robert in a desperate move to avoid speaking.

"Reshonaaa!" he bellowed.

Dropping my head even lower, I kept my mouth closed.

Offended and possibly a little tipsy, he got in my face. "Are you kidding me right now? Are you really *ignoring* me?"

I felt the stares of everyone there burning my skin. My face got hot. "No! I'm not. Hi," I whispered, tears threatening to spill from my eyes. Then I ran away.

Later at the studio, Robert chastised me. "Why didn't you just speak?"

"Because I thought I wasn't supposed to, Daddy."

"If you were *thinking* at all, you woulda just said hi. Instead, you made yourself look stupid."

In the beginning, Robert put so much energy into earning my trust and making me invested in what I believed was a real romantic relationship. So even as his demands became greater and so much started to not feel good, I was conflicted. What added to my confusion was that he made sure that some things felt good. Very good. After all, if everything felt bad, then I might have broken my resolve to take his secrets to my grave. Robert would treat me to nice things: shopping sprees, dinners out, going to the movies or some other fun thing, the latest sneakers, jewelry. Somewhere inside of me, I believed that a relationship was kind of like hazing. You grit your teeth and cry your way through the bad stuff to reap the good stuff. And Robert had the money, fame, and power to back up his words with lots of good gifts.

I know you see what I didn't. Part of his strategy was to buy my silence. But to me, he was showing me love. He'd taught me that we each had a role in our relationship. I gave him my body, mind, heart, and obedience. In return, he gave me my sense of value and worthiness, his professed love, a place of priority on his long list of sexual partners, public bragging rights with my friends and classmates, insider access to the music world, and the big-ticket gifts that my parents could never buy me.

I gave Robert all that I was. He gave me his crumbs. And every crumb had a receipt.

CHAPTER 6

RECEIPTS

ROBERT WAS BOTH MY drug and my drug dealer. I'd feel glorious in one moment and fearful in the next. He sometimes acted like I was his drug, too; he even used the alias of "Mary Jane" to refer to me. The highs felt amazing, and the lows were a lonely corner of hell. I was always scared: that someone would knock on the door, that someone would find out somehow. And I wasn't just afraid that we'd be caught in the act when it was happening. I was scared they'd see the videotapes.

Yes, *videotapes* with an *s*.

Once Robert hoodwinked me into doing something, he would videotape it. He taped everything.

"So you know I love how you lovin' me, baby."

He looked at me like there was more to say, so I waited.

"I don't want it to end. I don't want to lose it, you know." He nodded for me. "So we gonna be recording. From now on."

My body went cold, and my mind drew a blank. It was like I became a hollowed-out tree. I couldn't respond.

Robert's eyes were blue steel, but his lips made a little smile. "Ain't nothin' for you to do but do what I tell you to. You understand?"

I forced a sound from my throat. My mind ricocheted off the walls and my body felt like pins and needles.

"Then if I wanna feel you and you ain't here, I can watch, you know. But even more than that, Sho, it's for *you*. You know, to keep us safe."

What the fuck?

"Safe?" It was the only word I could get out, but I couldn't understand how making a permanent visual record of us doing things we didn't want *anyone* to know about would keep me safe.

Robert studied my face as if reading all the words in my head. "Baby, I know you tryin' to figure out what I'm saying. See, Sho, you know you can be a little loose with your tongue sometimes. I ain't hatin' you for it; I love you. You know that. But we gotta keep our secret. Am I right that you don't want nobody to see a tape of you sexing me up?"

"Yes, Daddy." I struggled to make sense of what he was saying.

"Right! That's what I'm talkin' about. These tapes will be like *motivation* for you to keep our secret. For you to never forget and let something slip by accident. Because you don't want nobody to see tapes of your titties or anything, do you?"

"No, Daddy."

"They're for my eyes only, Sho. I agree. And this way, I'll be sure that you won't make a mistake and say nothing. You understand me?"

"Yes, Daddy."

This was a totally different level of secrets. I was already scared about getting caught. And now this! I knew he wasn't careful with his things; he made others responsible for them. Whether it was his handlers who carried his cameras and gym bag full of homemade videotapes, or his housekeepers who washed his bedding and cleaned every surface in his studio and tour bus, dozens of people had daily access to the stuff of Robert's secrets. Robert ran his operation by requiring his staff to sign nondisclosure agreements to keep them from sharing what he knew they'd see. So how was he going to keep up with tapes of me? Dread weighed down on me like a bowling ball on my chest. I didn't know what blackmail was, but somewhere inside of me I felt that Robert was protecting *himself* by hanging me out to dry. I mean, I know I had let other people's secrets slip a time or two, but not *mine*. Not *this*.

As I tried to breathe through the pressure that was choking the air out of me, Robert went on with his explanation: Since I was young, *I* would be publicly shamed, and he would be punished if our love affair ever came to light. He would lose his career and his marriage. He made it seem like it was the two of us against the world because our love was real but frowned upon. I had heard this all before, but now his words took on new meaning. Even when I couldn't follow his rationale, I chalked it up to my naivete and trusted his experience. He had groomed me to trust him, obey him, confide in him, and I did. So, because Robert said this was the right thing for us, I told myself what he said was true. I had no idea that in a court of law, no matter how many times I said yes, it was still no because a child can't consent to sexual contact with an adult. I couldn't process that what he called a safety measure was completely reckless and added child pornography to the long list of problems with our so-called love affair.

Robert had taught me that our love fell outside of the bounds of what was common or expected, which was why it would scare other people and why it surprised even us. My seduced teenage mind couldn't reason like an adult's and poke holes in Robert's flimsy explanations. So, when Robert told me why he was going to film me, yes, I was hurt and scared. But it didn't make me run like my adult self would have. It didn't make me tell a teacher or my parents, because I was sure I'd be in trouble with them for all my lies, caginess, and especially sexual behavior. Robert had a narrow gate too, and while I couldn't be sure what God would do to me for disobeying *him*, I knew for sure that terrible things would happen if I didn't follow *Robert's* rules. My immediate fear of Robert caused my mind to make sense of his newest rule, reminding me that my big mouth had caused Aunt Sparkle to lose her record deal with Robert's label and may have cost her the career she had been building. Robert and I both knew I couldn't be trusted to keep quiet, so here I was, forced to swallow another of his rules that he said would keep us both safe.

At first, he would record sexual encounters, sometimes threesomes and sometimes just the two of us. Robert was very serious about his lighting and setup. He had multiple cameras attached to stands or the wall, and he purchased professional lighting so that his images would come out clearly. Then, if he was filming a threesome, for example, he'd have the two other people sit a certain way to perfect his angles and he'd have the camera lenses facing him so he could be sure he was capturing the action the way he wanted to.

Practically every sexual encounter was a performance, both in the moment and orchestrated for the purpose of creating a hardcore-porn video that he could get sexual gratification from later. For me, there was never anything pleasurable about having sexual encounters on demand.

Late one night, after Robert had stayed up most of the night making music, he came into the bedroom of the tour bus we were staying in.

"Get up, Sho."

"What?" I had been deep in sleep.

"Who you sayin' 'what' to? I'm horny, is what. You know makin' music gets me hard."

Everything made Robert hard. But I was asleep. And he smelled like weed, sweat, armpits, and almond-scented lotion.

"Just get me off quick and then you can return to what you were doing—"

"Sleeping—"

"And you better be dreaming about me."

"Yes, Daddy." I rolled my eyes and did what I was told.

This was *not* the quickie Robert promised. My eyelids felt like lead and everything he made me do annoyed the hell out of me. I couldn't believe he would wake me up from a sound sleep to get up close and personal with his funky ass. Damn.

When he was finally done, I rolled over and went back to sleep.

"Sho, wake the fuck up!" Robert poked me hard on my shoulder.

"Ow, Daddy." I rubbed the sleep from my eyes and pulled myself up to my elbows. As the scowl on his face came into focus, I felt a lump slide from the back of my throat into the pit of my stomach. I wanted to snatch my words back, but I couldn't.

"You lucky I'm just poking you with my *finger*!" Robert's eyes gleamed blue-black. "Get up and come here." He sneered at the fear in my face before standing back up and walking across the room.

A shiver ran down my spine. "But what's *wrong*?" I couldn't imagine what wrong thing I'd done while I was sleeping.

"Look at this shit." Robert's voice was low and tight. He pressed the little replay button on his video camera and started playing a video on the TV. "You were rolling your eyes the entire fucking time you were making the video! I couldn't even come to it!" Robert slapped the button, and my fed-up expression disappeared from the TV.

I stared at the dark screen, cold tears standing in my eyes. I was too upset to cry. I had been so tired that I didn't realize he was recording.

Robert punished me for that.

Many times when we were making Robert's videos, I was intoxicated. I never viewed the video that got leaked until I had to for the trial in 2022. It was so difficult to look at. As I watched Robert pour me glass after glass of Cristal Champagne, I could hear my speech slurring.

At some point, he said, "You know what I want to do to you?"

My mind was so soupy from the alcohol that I couldn't figure out how to answer.

Then he peed in my face.

I was shocked. Even through my intoxication, I felt disgusted and disgusting as he did it. I was still a virgin at that point, and I didn't know too much sexually, but I knew this felt horribly wrong. I didn't know how to stop him, though. He wasn't going to stop anyway; he was already doing it. I was just his puppet at that point. A puppet being fed more and more Champagne. God only knows if he had drugged the alcohol. Maybe he did. Either way, I was a fourteen-year-old girl who was one hundred pounds on my heaviest day, so the Champagne totally incapacitated me.

As disgusting as that one video was, it was not the most disgusting thing Robert did to me or required me to film of myself. For my own self-respect, I choose not to create a permanent record of those things in this book. I'm *not* protecting him. I'm protecting my peace. What I will say is I know that other women who were abused by Robert have shared stories about his willingness to use human excrement; my experience was the same.

Shame.

You spent so many years of your life ruled by that emotion: feeling responsible for wrongdoing. But the wrongdoing was done to you. Often done *through* you. Even now, the memories cause a pain that few can understand. It's too hard to wrap your mind around or to capture in words. Not that you would try. You refuse to assign language to your most abominable past horrors. For you, this is self-care. Others may see it differently. That's okay. You give yourself permission not to follow the crowd.

In all honesty, there is no crowd. So many who are quick to say what they would or would not do haven't been tested as you have. You know, from firsthand experience, what it's like to disguise yourself as the person you once were when your every vulnerability has been ravaged, when you have been so demoralized that your entire identity operates outside of your character. And you wonder whether his demons are yours too, because he chose *you* to do the unthinkable. Even the most understanding folks can't understand. You don't resent them, however. You wouldn't wish the reasons for the shame you carry on *anyone*.

Every day you lay it down. Every day you choose to release the shame. But emotions are tricky. They don't always go where they're sent. This is why you make compassion, for yourself and others, your daily practice.

Though Robert was turned on by disgusting things, sexual satisfaction wasn't the most important thing to him.

What made him able to jerk off to dehumanizing acts was his total control. If he could make you feel less than human, if he could show you that he had the power to make you do nasty, terrible, and despicable things to *yourself* or let him do them to you, then he had control over your *mind*, not just your body.

Robert used sex as a weapon of control. He was good at it. The videotapes were his receipts. I was scared that others would find those tapes, scared of what everybody would think if they saw them. But as I force myself to remember how fear poured from my skin like sweat, I now realize the scariest part was that he could abuse my body because he controlled my mind.

For me, fear, love, pleasure, obedience, and humiliation were one big feeling that overwhelmed me. It's why Robert could be my lover and abuser as well as my confidant and biggest protector. It's why I would lean my head on Robert's shoulder as he listened to me pour out my heart about the heaviness I felt inside.

"It's just, I hate lying to my parents. I mean, they love me."

"Of course they do."

"So then why, Daddy? Why does it have to be like this?"

Robert caressed my chin and lifted my head so I could see him. His smile was full of so much compassion and warmth that I rested in a temporary sense of safety. He kissed me lightly on the forehead and dipped his fingers into my tears.

"I hate to see you cry, Sho." Then he kissed my eyelids. "You know Daddy loves you."

I nodded. But my heart burned in my chest with all my conflicted feelings about the things he made me do and the rules he made me follow.

"What was that?" Robert responded to my silence, his voice a whisper and his face close to mine.

"Yes, Daddy." My voice was small.

"I know it's a lot for you, baby." Robert smiled again. "It's all so overwhelming. I get it. I feel like that too sometimes. That's why I make rules, Sho. They're for *you*, baby. To protect *you*. Because there's just so much that's new to you." He kissed me lightly on the lips and then on the tip of my nose. "You know Daddy loves you most of all?"

His expression full of anticipation, Robert waited for my answer. I knew what Robert said. I knew what I felt. But sometimes it felt like his love and protection required me to reject my parents' love and protection. After all, I lied to them all the time, but I hardly ever lied to Robert. Maybe this was love: choosing loyalty to your lover over an open and honest relationship with your mother, father, and baby brother.

"Sho, a father doesn't love his daughter like I love you. A father is just waiting for her to find a man who loves her more than he does. Then she'll leave her father and go make love and have babies with the man who loves her more than her father. I'm that man for *you*, Sho. I'm your daddy more than your father will *ever* be. That's why I keep telling you, 'Daddy loves you most and Daddy loves you *best*.' It's because I do."

I had been studying my fingers while Robert talked. My hands looked like my father's hands. *Your* hands, Dad. I was short like you, too. Your mini-me. I knew you loved me fiercely and unconditionally. You loved me because God made me, not for what you got from me.

But Robert made me full of more emotions than I had ever felt before. I felt *desired*. I couldn't imagine feeling more deeply connected to anyone than I did to Robert. And even though I wanted my father's good opinion of me, I cared more about what Robert thought of me. I didn't lie to Robert. I didn't hide my feelings from

Robert. At least not most of them. So maybe Robert was right. Maybe I loved Robert more, too.

"Yes, Daddy."

"It's you and me against the world, baby."

If the videotapes Robert made had been a woman, she would have been the only one Robert was ever faithful to. He kept his tape collection close; he'd have at least a dozen of them with him no matter where he went: in his gym bag, on his tour bus, and stacked behind his regular videotapes in his George Street house. With that many tapes, I guess it was no wonder that a couple might go missing. And when they turned up, they'd be duplicated many times over and hawked on the streets of every major city in America. Unfortunately, this was exactly what happened to me.

I didn't take any videotapes myself and, at the time, I wasn't sure who did. But lots of us knew he was making tapes because we were in them—being coached to do every explicit and demeaning thing for Robert's pleasure—and I'm sure I wasn't the only one who knew where the tapes were kept. I already knew that Robert would blackmail me with them if I ever decided to be disloyal to him. The biggest obstacle to me stealing a tape was fear, and I wouldn't have known what to do with it if I had taken one. But I guess that at least one person wasn't as scared as me, at least not enough to keep Robert's secrets forever. Maybe that's because they knew what to do with a tape once they took it. That half-hour-long tape of fourteen-year-old me made it to the streets. It also landed in the hands of my aunt Sparkle. And when she saw it, she called my parents to see what "we" were going to do.

The irony of this call wasn't lost on my parents, who were barely speaking to Aunt Sparkle after she called DCFS on them about two years earlier. Then, I had managed to lie successfully to Mom and Dad about those accusations (with Robert's help, of course). But now Aunt Sparkle had gotten ahold of a tape God only knows how, and had once again broken ranks with the family by planting the government into the middle of our family's business. This second accusation, in late 2001, was round two of the same terrible fight.

I was seventeen years old and the reason for my family's stress, and the source of the rift between Aunt Sparkle, my parents, and my extended family. Folks were Team Sparkle or Team Valerie, my mom. Our response to the three-year-old videotape felt like a doubling down on the same fear-driven strategy we used before: Don't air your dirty laundry for the world to see, and deny, deny, deny to wish away the bad stuff and save face.

CHAPTER 7

STRESS FRACTURES

YOU'RE TRYING TO REMEMBER. Trying to order the chaos that was your life into a logical sequence so you can digest it, retell it, and make it make sense. But that's not how you lived it. You never had the luxury of time or perspective to understand the mess you were in. Not you, not Mom, not Dad. You were all wading waist-high in a shit show, and in your desperation not to be pulled under, you became susceptible to every fear-driven scheme and short-sighted lie that masqueraded as a safety net and a place to catch your breath. Even though you were sick and tired of things, you still didn't have an adult's understanding that you'd been bamboozled. Did Mom and Dad know they'd been had too? You couldn't say. But in some ways, it didn't even matter. Their daughter was a pawn in a pressure campaign that could easily crush all of us.

I pressed rewind in my mind.

"Take all that shit off." Robert's voice was sandpaper against my ears.

We were in a windowless room on the second floor of the studio. As was often the case, the room was artificially bright from Robert's stage lighting. He positioned me so that several video cameras would capture every angle as I stripped silently. I removed my jewelry in addition to my clothes. Robert never wanted me to have anything that could be a weapon. Naked, I was hot with shame and hatred. I couldn't look at him.

"You know what this means? Now you're gonna get a spanking."

It was the summer of 2001, and I was nearly seventeen when Robert added this form of abuse to his list of responsibilities. The reason he gave for it was always the same: my disobedience. He was right about that; I wasn't going along with the program. I was fed up with everything: jealous of his marriage and all the other women that he kept around him, tired of constantly having to prove my love and loyalty, and frustrated by my inability to change things. The only thing I knew to do was to change my attitude and willingness to go along with his every whim. I started fighting him back. But in response, Robert's hands were fast and cruel.

"Come."

I shuffled my bare feet closer. But slowly. Robert could see my fear, my body tensing in anticipation of what was about to happen. He lifted my chin with his pointer finger, the hard ridge of his raggedy nail snagging my skin as he forced me to look into his cold blue-black eyes.

"Bend over." Robert positioned my naked body for maximum exposure and smacked my butt twice with his hand.

Pain radiated through me. I flinched as he tried to land the third slap and his hand missed.

"Don't move! Don't move!" Robert barked.

His voice sounded so theatrical that I imagined he must have been looking directly at one of his cameras when he said it. I squeezed my eyes closed and tucked my chin in tight to my chest. I wanted to deprive him of seeing my tear-streaked face when he replayed the videotape. Once he drew blood, he stopped. Tired from spanking me, Robert slowed his heaving breath that drowned out my whimpering.

Sometimes, the results of Robert's physical abuse upon my body would make him decide to keep me away from my family for a couple of days. I'd just lie to them and say I was having a sleepover with Andrea and the kids. If I still had a scar on my eye when I needed to be around my family, I'd lie my way out of it: "Oh, we were playing softball, and I got hit in the eye with the ball." I made my expression blank.

My parents studied me, their mouths pressed together in wordless concern. They didn't ask if we put ice on it. They didn't wonder why they weren't called to take me to the hospital. They didn't double back to Robert's door and quiz him about how our backyard ballplaying had resulted in my black eye. I waited for the questions that didn't come.

I was at the point where I was protecting a secret that I was praying would get out, but I couldn't find the strength to walk away. Then three things happened, one right after the other, that threw me back into Robert's arms. First, Aaliyah died in a plane crash in the Bahamas on August 25, 2001, and Robert was so devastated that he leaned on me for support. I was crushed too. Not only did I love her music and admire her as an artist, but since Aunt Sparkle had been a background singer for her and she had been an important person to Robert, my admiration for Aaliyah made me feel more connected to them both. Second, the 9/11 terror attacks happened, the tragedy announced over the intercom at my high school at the beginning of my sophomore year. Like so many kids, I was scared and confused; I couldn't make sense of it and felt like I needed Robert to help me calm down. And third, just a couple of weeks shy of my seventeenth birthday, the secret of my entanglement with Robert was exposed in the worst way imaginable. Robert told me that copies of one of the sex tapes of fourteen-year-old me were beginning to be sold on street corners in Chicago and across the country. Even though I hated that Robert was the reason why the tape existed in the first place, I was scared that facing the consequences without him would be more than I could handle.

Robert became my voice of reason and relative calm. He explained to me that we had to talk to my parents. He said he would profess his love for me, to them, that he would say sorry for lying but not sorry for loving me. And then, at the appointed time—he'd tell us when—Robert would insist that we leave the country for a while, for our safety and well-being, until the newness of this scandal died down. I was paralyzed by fear, but the sureness of his words felt comforting. At the time, it didn't matter that he would be asking my parents to lie right along with us. I let the mustard seeds of hatred that had only just started to take root inside of me scatter and die. Instead, I believed him when he said everything would be okay.

Robert told me how he would tell my parents the truth about us. He had his manager, Derrel McDavid, arrange a meeting at the Carleton of Oak Park Hotel. My mom and I were in one room and my dad and Robert went into the other. I never went into the other room, so I don't know if anyone else was in there with them. They stayed in there for a long time while my mom prayed and I cried in the other room.

After a while, Dad came storming out of the room, crying hysterically and cursing. "You're sick! I can't rock with you! I can't help you! You need to get help!" he yelled at Robert, who followed us into the elevator and was on his knees, crying.

"Man, I'm sorry. It's just that I love her!" He was begging for my dad to see things his way, telling him that he really loved and cared about me, and he didn't know how our whole love affair even happened.

Dad was not hearing it. Then Robert made a promise that we wouldn't have anything to worry about, that he would take care of me and us. I didn't know what all he and Dad had discussed in the room, but I knew what Robert said he would say: that we all needed to fall in line with his plan because he had thought through everything and had our best interests at heart. Robert didn't say all that in the elevator, though. Instead, he kept reminding Dad of what they had discussed in the room, begging him to see it his way.

The drive home was a blur of tears and disbelief.

You're too embarrassed to pick up your head and have Dad's eyes catch yours in the rearview mirror. You don't want to see your reflection in the window either. You turn your head away, rest it against the glass, and close your eyes. What did Robert tell your dad? Just the thought of it churns your stomach. Dad knows you've had sex. Dad knows you've had sex with a grown man. Dad knows you've been videotaped having sex with Robert, who peed in your face.

You open your eyes and look at your hands. They're not dirty, but they feel like it. *You* feel dirty. Is that how your parents see you now? Now that they know you're not the girl they raised you to be. And that you lied to them for years. You imagine they feel blindsided. You had raised your voice, cried, denied every suggestion that something was going on. You had called Aunt Sparkle crazy and lied to DCFS, too. What you can't imagine is that there must have been some willful ignorance on your parents' part, and that they believed your lies because they did not want the truth to be true. Your mind can't process that right now. All you can do is try to make yourself disappear into the back seat.

Your tears roll down your cheeks without making a sound. You realize Mom and Dad are silent too. They're not yelling at you. They're not even talking to each other. You steal a glimpse of Dad's face in the rearview mirror. His expression is as tight as a fist. Is he angry? Sad? Does he still love you? You can't see Mom, but her body heat radiates through the passenger seat and onto your knees. You are driving home. *Home.*

My parents prohibited me from seeing or speaking to Robert.

I was a chicken with my head cut off. Everything they asked me threw me into a panic. Unaccustomed to thinking for myself, I began my rampage. My body felt like it was on fire, so I was effective at hammering Robert's words into my parents' heads: "If you go against him, I'm gonna go against you. I'll kill myself!"

I didn't want to die, but I also didn't want to live without Robert and with the crushing humiliation that Robert told me was coming for me. I knew that my parents couldn't save me. Robert had explained that repeatedly, so the idea that they'd keep me away from him felt like an impossible existence. I knew that before I ever left Robert, I would escape my family so they'd never see me again, so I threatened them with that, too. On my seventeenth birthday, Robert suggested I start sleeping in my closet when I was at home. As miserable as that was, it was an escape.

With the revelation still fresh and my parents still forbidding me from seeing him, Robert devised a plan on how we could secretly get together. I'd cut school at whatever time he told me and drive my PT Cruiser—the car Robert had gifted me for my sixteenth birthday—to a parking lot in downtown Chicago. Then I would have to put on a wig to disguise myself, get out of my car, and switch to a rental car. I would drive the decoy car around a bit to make sure no one was following me before I drove to the Chicago Trax studio. I'd pull into that garage, get on the back elevator, and then run to one of the rooms.

Keeping up the charade of having gone to school, I was driving down the street in my neighborhood one afternoon when a group of young guys who were hanging out on the porch of a house started yelling, "R. Kelly!" repeatedly and laughing. My cheeks burned with humiliation. I wanted to flatten myself against the floor of the car, but all I could do was keep the car driving straight as I sped away. When I got home, I refused to tell my parents. Instead, I crawled into the bottom of my closet and whispered my despair to Robert. I was afraid to drive the car anymore, and Robert didn't want me to either. I don't recall where the PT Cruiser went, but from that point on, whenever I did leave the house, I drove an ever-changing assortment of rental cars.

I was deep into my rebellion when my parents pulled me out of my high school and made me a homeschooler. They explained that this decision was meant to shield me from the bullying and school-wide rumors that had my name all over them. Their impulse was right, but school wasn't my only problem. Yes, they had plucked me out of that fishbowl of stares, whispers, and snickers, but I had a bull's-eye on my back everywhere I went.

Shortly after all that, my family started packing for our Robert-dictated family trip. In all my secret conversations with Robert, he hadn't bothered to give me the heads-up. Instead, he had communicated this plan directly to my father. Apparently, it was the appointed time. As my dad explained it, Robert thought this was the best and safest option for us. It would keep us out of harm's way and give us an opportunity to wrap our heads around everything that was happening while also steering clear of the harassment of the media, private detectives, and law enforcement. I felt like I was a bobblehead, like my whole world had been cocked to one side. I no longer played with lil Greg and I responded to my parents' questions with gruff, one-word answers. And my withdrawal from Robert was giving me chills at night and a nonstop nail-biting habit during the day that made my fingers look like they had been gnawed on by a rat.

Under normal circumstances, the Bahamas and Cancún are great vacation spots, but our time there was agonizing. For one, sending my parents and me away actually pulled my family apart. Lil Greg, who was then nine, had to stay behind with our grandmother, Mom's mother, because he was in school. (I think we were gone at least a month, but being away from Robert had me so stressed that my sense of time was all jacked up.) Mom, especially, had a lot of uneasiness about this plan because she imagined his schoolmates would tease him about his sister's situation. I felt guilty about it, like I had failed lil Greg as his big sister, since I made him feel like he had to worry about and defend me when I should have been protecting *him*.

Mom and Dad did end up giving in to Robert's big demand: Fall in line and do what he told them to do when he told them to do it. I can barely remember all the conversations we had about our fucked-up situation, but we kept arriving at the same conclusion: Robert Kelly has money, power, and lawyers. We have none of that. This situation will crush us; it will embarrass me, drag our family through the mud, and drive a permanent wedge between my parents and me that could possibly end in my death. Not to mention that Robert's die-hard fans could harm one of us and the shady characters who worked for him could make any or all of us disappear.

My parents were a bundle of nervous tics, as if their bodies were being poked by a million invisible fingers. Before we returned to Chicago, Mom and Dad told me they had finished their months-long decision-making process and had come to a decision. To this day, I don't know what their process was. Their faces haggard and their voices frail, they explained that they didn't want to lose me or have me harm myself. They found themselves stuck between a rock and a hard place since I was now seventeen, the age of consent. They were as afraid for me as they were for themselves. So, while they disapproved of my relationship with Robert, against their better judgment, they would let me continue to see him. And since they didn't want me to go through any more public humiliation than I had to, they would follow Robert's lead. Their contradictory reasoning confirmed their own sense of powerlessness and their irrational hope that even though the sex tape was what got us to this place, perhaps the girl who was on it wasn't really me.

Their convoluted thinking made sense to me because I was in denial too.

When you're seventeen and lovesick for your grown and married secret lover, you cannot entertain any suggestion that your situation isn't good for you. That's why you still want his touch even though there's a bootlegged sex tape of you two for sale on the street corners of America. That's why you hate the person who leaked it more than the person who made it. And you let his lie seep into your soul. That girl is not you. That man is not him. If ever you worry about the sheer number of women he's slept with since you've been away, you believe him when he says their bodies are just stand-ins for who he really wants: *you*. You commit to being long-suffering in the name of your love.

It feels weird that your parents know your secret. Once upon a time, you thought that if they found out, your love affair would end.

Not too long ago, you wanted it to end. But now you're too caught up in the drama of the present to remember that part. New secrets have filled the spaces left by the old, and you're happy Mom and Dad now recognize the love you and Robert share.

Did my parents make a terrible decision? Maybe.

What I didn't fully know at the time was just how much Robert had sucked us into his tangled web and the financial hold he had over my entire family. My dad was a musician for him, he had invested in my mother's shoe store, and he strong-armed them into quitting their jobs so we could leave the country for a month or more. Robert became my family's only financial lifeline, which gave him receipts for all of us. I know that made it hard for my parents to see a way around the R. Kelly machine, which seemed bigger and stronger than anything we were coming with.

On the other hand, sometimes I think they saved me. Dangling suicide or an end to all communication with them was a cruel device Robert coached me to threaten. But it also made me consider these extremes as real possibilities. Suppose I had killed myself? Then they might have been right in the court of public opinion, but I'd be dead.

Scolded by our family and hiding from their friends, Mom and Dad swallowed every bitter pill Robert fed them out of love for me. They had made their bed in hell too. And it sucked. I mean, the misshapen ego of my seventeen-year-old self craved the devil I knew rather than the devil that Robert told me would surely find me if I broke ranks with him. But the little girl inside of me wished my parents could have been David to his Goliath and said, *Hell no, we're taking our daughter back!*

As a family, we closed ranks. My secret became a family secret and a loyalty test. Either you were for us—and willing to lie to protect me, bury our collective shame, and ignore the funky layers of codependence we had with Robert—or you weren't. Our family bonds that I once thought were unbreakable fractured at their point of weakness, splitting us in two. My parents and the family that sided with them—Team Valerie—repeated Robert's words, fed to them by the lawyers Robert hired for us and the band of strongmen who ringed him in a tight circle.

I watched my family fall apart, my emotions turned inside out. I wondered if taking myself out of this life would restore my family and give me peace. And would God have mercy on me if I did? Thankfully, I never learned what my threats of self-harm would have yielded. There was a perverse irony, however: Shortly after my parents and I perjured ourselves to an Illinois grand jury and linked arms with Robert in his big lie, we plunged into the deep end of hell. We would beg for God's forgiveness later.

CHAPTER 8

EVERYBODY'S SECRET

BECAUSE ROBERT AND I were continuing our relationship under the cloud of his twenty-one-count child pornography indictment, we couldn't even make the truth look true. I could no longer hide in plain sight as Robert's goddaughter. So he sent me underground, an effort that became an all-hands-on-deck operation in Robert's Chocolate Factory. I didn't have a bird's-eye view of what it took for Robert's plan to work. I didn't know what "it" was, what I would be required to do, how long it would last. But as I think back on those nearly seven years, the best way I can describe that time is that it felt like riding a roller coaster backward and blindfolded while the person at the controls slammed on the brakes whenever the mood hit him, whether I was upside down or at the top of a steep drop.

* * *

First, I moved into his Chicago Trax studio several months *before* Robert's June 5, 2002, indictment. Robert told me he had hand-selected a group of people he trusted and let them know I was around: studio manager Tom Arnold; personal assistant June Brown; musical director Donnie Lyle; sound engineers Ian and Abel; and his personal chef, Janet. He also told a lady who was a really good friend of his named Kathy, as well as his accountant and manager, Derrel McDavid. But those eight people were only the tip of the iceberg because Robert had a legion of folks milling around the studio as runners, assistants, engineers, musicians, business folks, bodyguards, and sex partners at every level. I was no stranger to these folks. They used to see me around all the time. But now I was the secret *everybody* was keeping.

Some knew my name and some my aliases. If I was hungry, I'd call down to order food under an alias name. (I ordered the same things that Reshona liked to eat using Reshona's same voice.) Then the person who was delivering it would knock a certain code knock at the door and leave the food on a tray on the floor. Some knew my face and some my wigs and sunglasses. If I needed to use the bathroom, I'd pee in a cup rather than leave the room. Or I'd put on a wig and run to the bathroom and then run back. (Not coincidentally, I was the same size and complexion as Reshona.) And if I needed to leave the studio and go somewhere, I'd put on huge dark sunglasses along with the wig and keep quiet.

I was too bogged down with misery, anxiety, secrets, and lies to question what Robert told me. But the word on the street was that at the very same time that Robert's ever-present goddaughter, Reshona, disappeared into thin air and he was being investigated for child sex abuse against that same girl, this new, shadowy presence showed up... behind a door. She was a dead ringer for Reshona from behind, if not for her blonde bob. You get the point, of course. Everybody working for Robert knew that it was me.

And then there were the people who knew my name and my face but who had their own complicated reasons for insisting they were ignorant of any relationship beyond that of my being Robert and Andrea's beloved goddaughter. I believe that my godmother, Andrea, fell into that category. I didn't know it then, but I certainly know now that she was preoccupied with her own domestic abuse at Robert's hands, and that he controlled her as much as anyone. A beautiful woman with a kind heart, she did show me the care and concern of a godmother earlier in our relationship. That's why I felt confused about her and Robert; it was hard to know how Andrea felt about Robert with other women and girls. Of course, as my grooming and abuse by him led me to have romantic feelings for him, my positive feelings toward Andrea morphed into jealousy. I thought I wanted what I believed she had.

There's so much more I could write about what I came to see and know about her abusive marriage, and I'm sure she could say the same about my child sexual abuse, but I won't. It's not to protect Robert or even her, but I recognize that she was likely operating in self-preservation mode for the good of their children. (Their oldest was fourteen years younger than I was, and Andrea was pregnant with their youngest when the indictments came down.) Unfortunately for Andrea, surviving her marriage—until she managed to escape it—meant choosing her battles with Robert. I imagine she just didn't have the bandwidth to process and address whatever she suspected or knew about my abuse within her home or outside of it.

I wasn't preoccupied with Andrea's hardships, however. Holed up in whatever room Robert had me in all day, I was consumed with enduring my own hellish existence. He would let me come out only if the studio was quiet and he was having a late-night session. Then I could sit in the session with him. Or sometimes he would have Janet cook us breakfast and we'd sit under a blanket in the back seat of his Hummer in the garage and eat it together. But despite these little moments of kindness and calm, I was miserable. We were fighting constantly because I was in hiding while Robert was dating other women whom he had made a priority over me.

Being trapped behind the black windowless walls of the studio robbed me of the sun and made the days run together in my head. It was always night in the 24/7 dreary darkness of the studio. How creativity could blossom anywhere in that maze of dark rooms was beyond me; I felt like I was withering.

Robert's answer to this was to get us a secret apartment downtown. The newness of the scandal had died down by this point, but the investigation was still dragging on, so Robert felt this was a good time to let the knowledge of me at the studio fade to black. What made the apartment a secret was that my parents didn't know about it. Even though I was technically still living under their roof, they knew me to be at the studio, so moving to an apartment would be yet another act of rebellion against them. I was still only seventeen at the time and had never lived anywhere alone, so it scared me to live in a downtown apartment by myself. Robert and I got into a big argument about it.

"I'm showing you my efforts, Sho, really being there for you, in your corner, and you ain't givin' me that same respect in return!" Blue glinted in his black pupils as if to mock me.

"But Daddy!" I squirmed. Backed up. My skin felt clammy. I

wanted to walk out of the room and away from our conversation, but there was no way he'd let me. His stare felt like he was dissecting every thought in my mind. *Defy my parents or defy Robert?* Both options thumped inside my head and made me sick to my stomach.

"Daddy what?" Robert's voice was nails on a chalkboard. "Look, Sho, we been over this a million times already. You keep tellin' me you're scared, but how you gonna stop being scared unless you fucking do it scared! Shit..."

"But suppose my parents catch me?"

"Then what, Sho? I mean, they know we in love, so they know we makin' love. What's there to catch? If you choosing me like I'm choosing you, then you gotta make them *respect* your choice!"

I gnawed at my thumbnail. This lie felt different. I guess it was because my parents were in on the *big* lie, and yet I'd be lying in their faces about where I was living. Of course, I didn't have to lie. Robert wanted me to be up-front and declare that I had chosen our relationship. That would *force* my parents to deal with my decision to live downtown as Robert's teenage mistress in hiding. After all, what could they do about it? They were following Robert's orders as much as I was. But this hit different. Before, my lie to my parents had been the *secret* of my relationship with Robert. He had trained me to lie through denial and deflection, and I knew how to do that well. But now that they knew about our relationship, I either had to put up my middle finger right in their faces or lie to Mom and Dad about where I was every night while still strong-arming them to protect my and Robert's relationship.

"Here I am, spending all this fucking money on a beautiful place you can be comfortable and safe in, and you just shitting bricks because you're scared. Then if I give the place up, what then?" He huffed and his hot breath covered my face. "What you're sayin' to me is stupid, Sho. Straight up. I'm not renting out some hole in the wall!"

"I know."

"And I'm serious as a heart attack right now."

The silence felt like a weight on my chest. I knew there was only one answer. "Yes, Daddy."

"Good. Took you long enough." Robert called June Brown to tell him. "She said yes!"

June was silent as he brought in my things and helped me to get settled in. I didn't speak to him either, since Robert forbade us from conversing. I wondered if he could tell how upset I was about my predicament. The apartment was nice, but because I was sneaking to stay there, right under my parents' noses, I always felt uneasy. I started spending time at the apartment without fully living there. I still preferred being at the studio because it was an environment I was more familiar with, even though it was dreary and claustrophobic. I guess he eventually got rid of the apartment, and then I moved into his tour bus, which was parked at his Olympia Fields home, the massive mansion that was then his primary Chicagoland home.

Anniversaries remember.

The years 2002 through 2008 remain a dead zone in your memory. The run-up to Robert's indictment through the end of his trial more than six years later is stuck in a fog of hurt and shame. Even now, as you try to untangle the web of those years, some memories zigzag through the dead zone. Out of order and raggedy. The half-rotted corpses of pain and humiliation sleep in shallow graves, unable to find dates on a calendar.

You make your mind a safe space for good memories. But still, you must be careful. Not all memories about Robert are bad. And with the bad memories buried, the good memories can push up daisies. Trauma makes you want to revise your past, but you will not let your mind be a garden of beautiful lies. So you revisit the graves only long enough to let the ghosts out.

I'm reclaiming that time, but *not* the trauma.

Each day was a nagging repetition of the day before, punctuated only by Robert flipping the script on me whenever it suited him. With no friends outside of Robert, no stability, and no sense of self, I was losing my grip on reality and wondering if God even remembered my name. It was with this frame of mind that I was completing my junior and senior years of high school as a homeschooler in 2002 and 2003.

On paper, homeschool was my parents or my cousins (who were licensed teachers) teaching me the curriculum laid out by Christian Liberty Academy. The first time I was homeschooled was when I was with 4 The Cause, and it was certified through the CLA program. This time, however, I was largely left to my own devices to progress through my lessons. Robert provided me with a cell phone, but he monitored all my calls and text messages. There was a very short list of approved numbers I could call or text to ask a question if I needed help; if those calls lasted too long, or if the text thread veered off topic, Robert would question and discipline me for it, sometimes with a spanking and sometimes by withholding food or bathroom privileges. I knew that Robert didn't handle his own bills, though; Derrel did most of that. So Robert must have had someone else reviewing and flagging stuff for him. Even with those challenges, I held on to my parents' dream of seeing lil Greg and me graduate high school, along with the doses of encouragement my cousins offered me. School was one of the few things that kept me putting one foot in front of the other. Determined not to fail, if I got stuck on something, I would hunt for resources. But the physical and emotional constraints of my circumstances kept it from being an enriched education. I was pretty much just getting by, and unfortunately, I still have some of the learning gaps I developed then.

I wasn't allowed to see my family or the few friends I still had, even on holidays. Most of my and Robert's arguments and fights and his abuse of me stemmed from me hating this part of him that seemed happy to make me miserable. So Robert came up with his latest effort to plant insecurity and jealousy deep inside of me: He decided to pair me with one of his newest sexual partners, a young woman I'll call Alyssa.

I was jealous of her, and she was jealous of me too when we first met, mostly because that's how Robert liked to do it. He always played one woman off the other, so we'd compete to be his best girl rather than see each other as allies. Since I didn't have any friends or anyone I could relate to, Robert would send the two of us out to shop or run errands. She later told me that, shortly before she and I first went out, Robert had broken down crying in her lap, confiding how much he loved me and that he feared he had ruined me. Because of that experience, she knew there was something different about me. She explained that she had a soft spot for me. We became cool, and over time, I really valued her friendship.

When I shared some of the negative dynamics of my relationship with Robert, she had a quick comeback. "I wish he *would*! He knew who to play that with!" Alyssa had already spelled out to me that no part of her life required Robert's approval. Walking into their situationship with both eyes open and on her own terms, Alyssa wasn't afraid to assert herself with Robert.

"I wish I could be like you." My voice was wistful.

"Girl, shit! Then be like me." Alyssa pursed her lips. "I'm not gonna lie, Shon. I can't hardly imagine Robert acting mean or controlling like you say he does to you. I mean, I'm not saying you're lying... but—I mean, this man cries in my arms about you." She hunched her shoulders. "I just can't see it, is all I'm tryin' to say."

"Just because you can't see it, don't mean it's not happening." I stared straight at Alyssa to force her to hold my stare. "When you started messing with Robert, you were already a whole damn woman. What were you? Twenty-one, twenty-two?"

"Yeah, about that."

"And you already had a job and paid your own rent?"

"Okay, so?"

"So I was eighteen when I met you, and I'd been with Robert for five years already."

"Damn, Shon." She seemed amazed.

"You know how to stick up for yourself, how to not take shit from him and make him respect you. I can't do that. He'll just shut me down! I mean, I bet you don't depend on him for one thing in your life!"

"I don't mind spending *all* his Benjamins!" Alyssa laughed, and I joined her as she pretended to scatter hundred-dollar bills from a tall stack of cash. "But you right, though. Robert's money is play money for me."

"Seriously, Alyssa, you could walk out this door just as easily as you walked through it and you'd still know exactly who you are!" I felt like I had finally made a point. I searched her face, looking for understanding.

"See, that's where you lost me, girl. I mean, even if you see a darker side of his messy ass than I do, you still a whole damn woman, same as me. You're still you: beautiful and smart too. And anybody with eyes can see you got all your goods in full working order!" She chuckled and bounced her behind for emphasis. "So act like it, you know!"

I couldn't laugh with her this time. She didn't get it. "It's just not that simple, Alyssa."

"Girl, look. I'm not saying Robert's perfect. He sure as hell wouldn't know how to be faithful if somebody put a gun to his damn head." We nodded our agreement. "But even if he can be an asshole sometimes, maybe you're making some of the shit between y'all hard. I mean, he seems to be hooked on whatever you got between your ears *and* your legs. So if he wants some of that good-good, make him work for it! That's it."

"Yeah." Alyssa had more faith in Robert and me than I did. I decided not to say more.

Some of the arguments between Robert and me were about her. I fussed that if he could treat her right, he could do the same by me. But I learned the hard way that what he *could* do and what he *would* do were two completely different things. And unfortunately for me, I had banked my entire life on him, and he had groomed me—and my parents—in a way that Alyssa would never have allowed. That's why he never felt like he had to treat me any better than he did.

Though our friendship has outlived my relationship with Robert, I have to be careful not to overshare with Alyssa, since she may still be in contact with him. I know that she thinks Robert was just conforming to the evils of the music industry and that music executives didn't have a problem with him until he started trying to buy back his masters and mess with their money. But to my mind, you can't make a man's faults, demons, and predatory behavior toward young women and girls just a problem with the industry, as messed up as it is.

Alyssa, even though you have some blind spots when it comes to Robert, I still appreciate our unexpected, organic friendship; it was a saving grace that came at a time when I needed it most. What Robert meant for evil became something good for us. You cared about me without hurting me, always showed up for yourself and took up space, and gave me a down-to-earth model of how to be a whole person in romantic and sexual relationships.

For my twenty-first birthday, Robert gave me a tiny break from what was basically house arrest and threw me a Robert-approved dinner, complete with his handpicked guest list that included a few of my family members, along with folks who were loyal to him. My guests were happy to see that I looked well, and I got false hope that things were looking up for me and for us. I couldn't have been more wrong. My happy day notwithstanding, it was also the month that Andrea left Robert, and Robert's attitude toward me became even more hateful.

When things were especially bad, Robert would sometimes slip me a short, handwritten note or a drawing as an unstated apology that let me know he was thinking about me. It must have been late 2005 or early 2006 when I heard paper sliding under the door of the room I was trapped in. I walked over to pick it up: three and a half handwritten pages in one long paragraph that had been torn from a lined notepad. I knew the handwriting wasn't Robert's; he wasn't good at writing or spelling, and whenever he wrote from his own hand, it was always large and in all caps. But I recognized the broad, even print as belonging to Abel, one of the sound engineers Robert trusted the most. Robert must have dictated his thoughts to him. When I read it, Robert's message was convincing.

He told me that he knew his words weren't matching his actions, but he wanted me to know how in love he was with me and that the feelings he had for me hadn't changed. He explained that the industry had gotten more competitive, and then his new songs had been bootlegged, so he was stuck in the studio recording a whole new album. He wanted to assure me that it wasn't personal, but his comeback to the industry was. He knew it was difficult for me to understand, but he tried to give me as much comfort as he could. "It's been seven years of hell," he wrote, with his wife leaving him, dealing with threats against him, and claiming that he was being blackmailed by Bruce, Killa, the Henry Loves, and everyone else who betrayed him. He said that all this going on while he was fighting for his life in court was the worst thing that could happen to anybody... that the only thing that could be worse was death itself.

I could only imagine dealing with all that while he felt his life was on the line court-wise, so I sympathized with him. He didn't want a pity party; he just wanted my understanding and confidence in the love he had for me. He explained that he needed to keep girls around him in the studio because he fed off the way they loved him, and it helped him be more creative. He promised me that no matter what was going on at his parties, what people he was spending time with, or where he was in the world, he would always find his way back to me. He reminded me that he had promised himself seven years before that as long as he held on to me and held on to his music, he would come out on top. He finished by saying that I always was and would always be his "full moon." I believed him.[1]

I folded the letter in quarters like it had arrived and squeezed my eyes closed. I tried to imagine Robert dictating his words to Abel. Did he look back at Robert in disbelief when Robert said he was fighting for his life and couldn't imagine anything worse than what *he* was going through, short of death? Did it occur to Robert that I was going through hell too? Did he really expect me to feel bad that Andrea, aka Drea, finally left him, or sympathize with his need to fuck some random women so he could be creative? So many of Robert's words stung me down to the bone. But then I thought about his bold-faced declarations of love. What did Abel think of those words meant for me? My mind and body—so starved for affection and just the stimulation of living out in the world—tingled with the thought of Robert saying those words so that Abel could write them down. Robert wasn't ashamed of saying he loved me, and that felt good.

I tried not to compare Robert's hardships to my suffering. What was the point? I wasn't going anywhere. I wasn't going to do anything different. It sucked. Everything sucked. But what could I do about it? I was around twenty-two at this point, and I had chosen to lie in this bed, even if I hadn't been the first one to make it. Bogged down as I was with my own misery, I couldn't let my mind stretch enough to think about how things started. I was just fighting to stay grounded in the present. And that meant tossing one more insult upon the pile of injury that came with loving Robert.

* * *

As we waited for the trial to begin, Robert redoubled his commitment to making sure my life was as narrow and dependent upon him as possible. That's why he controlled my access to other people, especially my family. It wasn't that I never saw or spoke to any family members ever, it was that Robert dictated who I could see, when, where, and how freely I could talk to them. Communication with every approved relative was heavily monitored. I couldn't communicate or be cool with any males in my family, outside of my father. And since Robert was on the outs with Sparkle, that meant he had strained relationships with the entire Edwards side of my family. That's why I had limited access to them.

The Landfairs were a different story. Robert had met Grandma Ruby—Dad's mom—early on when Dad started playing for Robert. Grandma Ruby was a meek and matronly Southern gentlewoman who didn't need a reason to make you a German chocolate cake from scratch. Robert was the happy recipient of many such cakes. So, even as things got tense with me being in hiding, Robert still had a soft spot for Grandma Ruby.

I can't say how genuine Robert's feelings were for the other Landfairs, but as the master puppeteer, he knew that positive connections with Dad's family would keep Dad in check and maintain tension between him and Mom. These complicated relationships were the backdrop for who Robert allowed me to connect to. Grandma Ruby was the cream that floated to the top: the one female family member he'd allow to come to the house to visit me. She could come over to cook. And she could talk about the food she made. That was basically it.

Sometimes, when I was hiding in the studio, I'd hear him having big parties. People would come around to where I was and knock on the wrong door, and all I could do was listen to the world moving on without me. This happened less often when Robert turned the garage of his Olympia Fields mansion into a boxing gym and moved me into that, but I would still be taunted by the arrival of Robert's guests: entry gate creaking open, tires crunching the gravel as car after car rolled up the driveway, headlights flooding my room in white light. (I was not supposed to peek but sometimes I did.) Following his separation, when Robert moved me into the office space of the main house, I could hear the music and sometimes smell the food and drinks on the other side of the door. I complained to Robert about his cruelty; it was as if he wanted to punish me more than protect me. In response to this, Robert would have June inform me that I was going to be temporarily moved to a hotel within a one-mile radius of the Olympia Fields house: the Holiday Inn down the road, the Homewood Suites, or the Courtyard by Marriott. That's how I knew Robert was going to have a party. While I wasn't constantly taunted by the fun that I was barred from, I also knew I'd miss my dad.

Dad knew where I was living in the Olympia Fields house. Whenever Dad was working at the studio on the lower level, an area that included the studio, a theater, and a couple of bathrooms, he would text me and then slip into the house, to the bathroom that was off-limits. Or he would surprise me and do it. If he and Mom were at an event at the house, he would sneak around to where I was and knock his own special knock very lightly, and I'd let him in.

He'd ask, "Are you okay? Do you need anything?"

No, I'm not okay. I need to be saved! I feel like I'm cracking up! I looked into Dad's eyes. There were no good words to say. Dad's concern for me wasn't going to change anything, unless he was planning to snatch me up and haul ass out of there.

Dad wiped at his eyes before tears spilled from them. "Your mom and lil Greg are okay. Folks at the music school think he's a prodigy the way he's tearing it up on the drums." Dad forced his lips into a smile.

I wanted to do the same, but my lips kept trembling. Robert had started monitoring my conversations with lil Greg after he turned thirteen and limited when I could see him, so it was hard to picture him as taller than me now and hear a deeper version of his little-boy voice. It was almost like he was frozen in time for me. Remembering how Robert used to support lil Greg and me bonding by giving me money to take him shopping, I felt bitter that I no longer knew his style or what he liked to do. As Dad described his baby-hair mustache and how proud he was that lil Greg was finding his musical voice—even forming a band with his friends at his Saturday music school—I regretted missing lil Greg's teen boy glow-up. I was missing *everything*. But maybe he wasn't missing me.

Dad sat with me for a little bit longer, listening to me breathe, watching me cry silently. Then he hugged me and went back to whatever he was doing like nothing happened.

It was at this time that my love for Robert turned into hatred.

I hate that I love you, whatever the fuck that means. You made me addicted to you. You corrupted my mind and body to feel like I need you the way an addict needs their pipe. Is that love? You tell me you love me, and I want to believe you. But this feels like shit. You demoralized me, made me a cesspool for every depraved thing you could think to do with me and to me. You made me believe that my body and mind were created for you. *That love means I will always be whatever you want me to be.*

I'm in so deep that I don't know anything else. I don't know what I want, what I feel, who I can be. I've put in so much time and lost so much that's important to me that I don't want to lose you, too. My identity is who I am to you, and I hate myself for it. How can I love a man like you? You've been despicable to me.

Am I partly to blame for the monster you are? Because I was a little girl who didn't fight you? Because I learned to be everything you wanted? But that's not even true! You trained me, and yet I'm not enough. Your dick still finds whatever hole it wants to fuck, and I sit here in this room wondering what's wrong with me*!* Is she prettier? *I wonder.* Smarter? *I've been comparing my body and mind to grown women's from the time I was thirteen years old.* You *taught me to do that. But these grown women were* never *my peers.* You *were never my peer. You've fed me lies, made me jealous and insecure, and used my youth against me and in service to you.*

Look, Robert, I'm sorry about your fucked-up childhood. Little Robert didn't deserve to be used and abused like you were. But adult Robert used his God-given talents and became a star, in spite of all that. And rather than healing the pain of the little boy you were and seeking help for your addiction, you chose to ruin me and threw some others in there for good measure. You did it because you could*! Because your money and fame meant no one would stop you!*

And now, I don't exist. I'm a ghost sitting behind a door waiting for you to remember I'm here. Everyone else has forgotten me. Moved on with their lives. Who do I have left but you?

I was far from shore and too tired to swim. Even though Robert was the reason I was drowning, he was the only boat.

Robert's insistence that he control everybody's access to me shaped what I knew about the case being mounted against him. He made sure I was ignorant of everything else. He would put so much spin on every piece of information before he fed it to me. That way, just like a ventriloquist, he could stuff words into my mouth for whenever I managed to sneak in an unsanctioned conversation or text exchange with a family member. This was how Robert was able to pull all the strings in my extended family.

One major aspect he impacted was how I thought about Aunt Sparkle. When Robert did let me come out of hiding long enough to spend some quality time with him, one of the things he liked to talk about was his haters who were dead set on taking him down. The two people at the top of that list were Aunt Sparkle and Barry Hankerson. Barry was his former manager as well as the uncle and manager of the now-deceased Aaliyah. He was sure that Barry saw Aaliyah's untimely death as Robert's fault, even though she was no longer his artist when she died. Robert never talked about how he started a sexual relationship with Aaliyah when she was thirteen and illegally married her in 1994, when she was fifteen and he was twenty-seven. Instead, he talked about what a bad manager Barry was, claiming that he stole money from him and held a grudge against Robert for cutting off their toxic professional relationship and the future earnings from Robert's success that Barry felt were his.

Of course, things ended badly between Robert and Aunt Sparkle, too, and she moved from Robert's label to Motown, an arrangement that Barry helped to facilitate. Her album with Motown didn't do nearly as well as the one she made with Robert, so Robert said this was why she wanted to get back at him, too. He kept drilling into my head that Aunt Sparkle was out for money and revenge, and that she was willing to sacrifice me to get it. This theory became a part of the air I was breathing under Robert's control. When I heard him tell it, it seemed to make sense. And I believed that she was angry with me, too, so maybe she was willing to sacrifice me to get her revenge against him. Robert said Barry and Aunt Sparkle were in cahoots to sabotage his career because of the axes they each had to grind.

A version of this same theory made the rounds within my family as well, because of the strained relationship between Aunt Sparkle and my mom. My parents had cut off my relationship with Aunt Sparkle completely after the videotape surfaced. That, combined with my limited access to my family and my steady diet of half-truths and self-serving spin from Robert, shaped my thoughts about everything, convincing me that Aunt Sparkle was a bad actor in this whole deal. Whatever filtered to me from my family on the rare occasion when I would get to see them seemed to match up with what Robert told me: Sparkle was a bad person who was willing to take the family down. As an adult, I have come to realize there were many layers to the murky mess of Aunt Sparkle's early career with Robert. He had his own reasons for feeding me his narrow slice of that story. But the truth was a whole cake.

I was surprised when Robert showed me his willingness to sacrifice his own brother's freedom for his own. One day, when we managed to find some time together, Robert was venting and telling me some of the tactics he and his lawyers were batting around as they developed their defense of his innocence.

"You know, as me and my lawyers were talking and they asked me if the dude in the video could be anybody that maybe, you know, looked like me, I realized something. He looks like a dead ringer for *Carey*."

"Carey?"

"You know, my younger brother." Robert sniffed. "Shit, the dude coulda been *anybody*, really! Any brown-skinned tall nigga, anyway." Robert looked at me. "But especially Carey. I mean, we look the same! We identify in the same way!"

I was stunned. Robert had a self-satisfied smirk on his face like he had made a discovery. Though I was sitting still, in my mind I was running through a house of mirrors. I couldn't be sure Robert was being real with me.

He hadn't seemed to notice and was still talking about the video, which he called the alleged video. "I don't even *watch* that shit. Like, I don't hardly know what's even on it."

"It's *us*."

"Don't fucking say that, Sho! You don't even know what's on there."

Of course we knew. Robert and I both knew that it was fourteen-year-old me on that tape, following everything he told me to do and say. And now he was telling *me*—the person who lied under oath about my own identity to protect *him*—that the man who peed in my face could have been *anyone*, up to and including his brother. I felt disgusted all over again. To add insult to injury, Robert was dissociating himself from the video, suggesting that he didn't even want to watch it and never did. As if that mattered.

I said nothing, again. Somewhere inside, I wished that I could have come back with something Alyssa would have said, but I knew that might have gotten me popped in my mouth, or worse.

So much of how I thought about my life and the people around me was deeply rooted in the lies Robert told me. *Carey's a bad person. Barry, Sparkle: bad people. And Mom needed to be put in check.* He made up a whole world for me in which he was my hero, my god even, who was always working behind the scenes to make things better for me.

In order for him to be the good guy, there had to be bad guys, and for a teenager and young adult, the people in your world are your family and friends. So he tried hard to make me believe that nobody was as concerned about me as him. That nobody loved me as much as Robert did, with Dad in second place. But even my dad couldn't take care of me the way that *he* could. So, since this was the case, the only truth that mattered was whatever made Robert the hero.

One way he made himself my hero was by punctuating my life with a highlight reel of big gifts and lavish celebrations: from a PT Cruiser for my sixteenth birthday and letting me attend my grandmother's big sixtieth birthday bash, to a limousine for my high school graduation and fancy parties for my eighteenth and twenty-first birthdays when I was underground. There were also gifts that were hidden in plain sight: the lyrics from his songs. Probably the most well-known line is from the backyard-barbecue and family-reunion anthem of the world, "Step in the Name of Love": *"If anybody asks why we did it, tell them that we did it for love."* He even wrote a whole song for me, "Butterfly," on his *Love Letter* album, because of my love for them. Some of the lyrics he wrote while being intimate with me.

Those quiet or lavish gifts gave me life at the time. They were like confirmation that there was something good, right, and true about our relationship even though it often felt wrong or painful. I realize now that even the sweetest things were ultimately manipulative. You remember riding that roller coaster backward and blindfolded? Well, Robert knew that if I never got off, I'd die, and if he ran it for too long and stopped it, I would escape and tell everyone about how terrible it was. So he had to keep me in his pocket: punishing, but not so punishing that I wouldn't care about the consequences of spilling every single bean. He was no longer grooming me; now he was maintaining me. He upped the pain and the pleasure in unequal measure. That way I stayed off-balance, emotionally drained, and grateful for every minor show of kindness. That was just where he wanted me to be.

CHAPTER 9

BAD, GOOD, AND UGLY

ROBERT MADE ME STOP talking to Mom for more than a year.

Several months into our forced silence, my dad called me. "What's going on with you and your mom? Why aren't you talking to her?"

Because I can't, Dad. Do you really have to ask? "No reason."

"No reason?" Dad sighed. "Look, I don't know what's going on between you two, but like, she's getting really sick, Reshona. She's starting to lose her hair because she's so stressed out that you're not talking to her."

"I'm sorry to hear that, Dad." I made my voice calm and unemotional. I couldn't give him an explanation, but I also wasn't up for the fight with Robert that would surely come if I got myself too worked up on the phone. So I didn't. I shut down instead.

"Well, do you have a message for her?"

"No, I don't."

"What should I tell her?"

"Whatever you want, Dad. Whatever you want."

Dad was at a loss for words and so was I.

"I have to go, okay? Bye." My stomach squeezed and gurgled. I sat still, hoping not to throw up. I couldn't afford to get sick. Who would help me?

As I calmed my body, my brain pressed rewind, stopping at about six months before. Robert had come to spend time with me and tell me about Mom's latest infraction. "You know your mom and dad came to my party last night."

I knew because Dad had paid me a secret visit. But I raised my eyebrows in surprise.

"Yeah, and your moms was trippin', acting like she wanted to curse me out or something. She was frowning at the other girls who were, you know, around me and shit. Like, why she tryin' to disrespect me like that? And Sho, if she's disrespecting me, then she's disrespecting *you* too. I mean, you're not a child. You're a grown-ass woman. This is *our* environment." He threw his hands wide. "If she don't know how to fix her face in our environment—" He didn't finish his thought. "I mean, shit! How she gonna come in here and call attention to you and make you look bad?"

How did I look bad? I wasn't even there. "You didn't say what she was frowning at." My mind started to paint a picture of the party: the food, the drinks, and especially the guests.

"See, that's what I mean, Sho. You still acting like some goddamn child. I don't give a fuck what she saw. She don't come to a party I'm throwing and mess up the energy in our environment like that. That's why you need to show her she can't be doin' that shit."

I couldn't follow Robert's logic. It wasn't my environment because I wasn't there. I wasn't the hostess. I wasn't even a guest. I was trapped in a room, hidden from the world.

"Sho, you gotta teach her to respect you, respect *us*."

I still couldn't see the us in the situation. Mom probably got her nose out of joint because Robert had all these girls riding his dick. She probably felt disrespected... for herself and for me. Waves of jealousy derailed my rational thoughts. All I could see were young women with flimsy dresses and no underwear hugging up on Robert and him tweaking their nipples or French kissing them without a care for who might see him. In fact, he might have done it specifically for Mom to see. My face grew hot.

"Now you have to treat her with the same lack of respect she showed me so she can get over herself. You need to take some time off from her and make her feel uncomfortable."

I tried to flush that image out of my brain. I looked at Robert. "What do you mean?" *Time off?* I didn't even get to visit her. How could I take time off from her?

"Haven't you been listening to me, Sho? You need to ice her out. Stop talking. Then she'll learn her lesson."

My brain throbbed with the memory of treating Mom worse than I would a person on the street. I didn't know when Robert would finally lift this restriction, but I was scared to ask. It was another total mindfuck. And judging from what Dad said, it messed Mom up, too.

As bad as that was, though, that kind of thing happened all the time. Like I've said before, Robert liked to use folks' personalities and vulnerabilities against them and then squeeze himself into the crevices of folks' relationships to sow discord. He didn't spare my parents. He used me as the pawn that made them ask, "How high?"

when he said, "Jump." But though he manipulated them both, he had completely different approaches for each of them.

Since Dad had a good working relationship with Robert as his guitarist and was a completely nonconfrontational guy, Robert liked him. Dad probably saw stuff at the studio that even I didn't know about. It's not to say Dad was cool with everything he saw, but he was able to play it cool and keep a poker face. Some might say this was a fault, and maybe sometimes it was. But I think it's what allowed Dad to stay connected to me during all my hard years. I inherited Dad's poker-face gene, and it's how I survived too.

Mom was completely different. You're going to know how she feels about stuff. Either you'll see it on her face, or you'll hear it in how she answers you. Whenever Robert wanted to use me against my parents, he coached me on how to punish them through my relationship with my mom.

Robert's stranglehold on my parents became a full-blown financial dependency because my dicey situation made it damn near impossible for them to cover our family's expenses. Dad played guitar for practically every artist and event that rolled through Chicago, but he had no nest egg to show for it. Before she opened her shoe store, Mom held a job that wasn't a career. We were Black middle class on our best day. So when Robert told Mom and Dad they needed to leave their jobs and the country for a month or so in order to sidestep all the journalists and investigators trying to get their story, they choked. But when the media started crowding into the reception area of the office where Mom worked, things changed. Not only had their jobs become a liability for the lie we were all trying to tell, but Mom turned into a liability for *her* job too.

Under tremendous financial and emotional strain, Mom and Dad became financially dependent upon Robert. They would ask him for money to help with things like lil Greg's school tuition, our mortgage, or to keep Mom's shoe store afloat. My parents didn't talk to me about it; Robert did. And he always took every opportunity to belittle them in my eyes.

"Sho, I'm sick of your mom blowin' up my phone talking about their money problems. 'Rob, we need this, Rob, we need that!' Look, your dad's cool, but what the hell is wrong with your parents?"

They did what you told them to. "But isn't that what you agreed to, Daddy?" I didn't want to say too much.

He sidestepped the question. "They were the ones who decided to have you and your brother. Seems they forgot it would cost money to raise y'all!" Robert snickered.

"That's not fair, Daddy!"

"What's not fair is expecting me to pay for a lifestyle they clearly can't afford. R. Kelly *pays* his goddamn bills!"

What lifestyle? "They're trying!"

"They ain't tryin' hard enough. Also seems you forgot who's team you're on, Sho." He stared at me. "If you're gonna be on my team, you have to do things *my* way so your parents can understand how things go."

I'll be frank: My parents had financial issues. Unfortunately, Robert knew this, and he was able to exploit them because of it. I know that many people have aired their opinions about my parents' decisions and have accused them of selling me out. While hindsight is 20/20 and I can agree that my parents didn't always make the right decisions, I can say with confidence that they didn't see me as their cash cow without a care about what happened to me. It was far more complicated than that. My parents made the mistake of thinking that every path to musical success in Chicago went through R. Kelly and that he was too big a giant to be taken down. But more fundamental than what they believed about Robert was what they believed, period. Even though they were lifelong Christians, Mom and Dad were operating in fear instead of faith.

It was sometime around my twenty-third birthday when Robert lifted his ban on me speaking to Mom. I know it seems weird that I can't remember exactly when that hellified requirement ended, but it's like my mind won't let me. It's another memory that's too painful to give an anniversary to. And I can say the same for my mom. We have agreed to let some of the specifics of that time in our lives die so we can keep living. When I finally did call my mom, she was so hungry to hear my voice, and so scared that one false move would plunge us back into the same predicament, that she didn't ask any questions about it.

What I didn't know was that we were getting closer to the beginning of Robert's trial. The date may have even been set by then, though he didn't tell me. By this point, I was actively hating him about 65 percent of the time, so it took everything within me to try to keep my cool around him. I failed at that most days; we were having arguments and fights on the regular.

Robert must've figured that now was a good time to get me feeling more positively about him and remind me of the pros of being whatever the hell I was to him. One night, he invited me to a midnight breakfast in his Hummer. There, he made an announcement: I deserved some fun, so he would treat my mom, two of my cousins, and me to a weeklong trip to Miami!

I was so grateful for this opportunity to leave the box I had been living in, let the sun warm my skin, and hug Mom in person that I didn't question whether Robert had an ulterior motive. I just jumped at it. The two cousins I invited, Shonna and Shontae, were a little older than me and were among the family members Robert had deemed "loyal" enough to me—and him—that he felt they could be trusted. (On the very few occasions when I had successfully begged Robert to allow a few of my female relatives to come visit me at the house since I couldn't visit them, Shonna and Shontae were on the short list.)

By every measure, the trip was great. Robert's team booked first-class airplane tickets and a cushy suite at a high-rise resort. One day, while Shontae and I were getting a little exercise, we walked past a pet shop. I fell in love with a doggie in the window. This was a big deal for me. I didn't grow up in a pet-loving family, but it was like I needed the love that only a dog could give me. We went inside. The dog—*my* dog—must have recognized that I was his person, too, because he looked at me with his puppy-dog eyes and played puppy games with me until I said yes.

I called Robert to ask if I could get him and he agreed. He sent me the money. Shontae named him Buddy because that was exactly what I needed. Buddy, who was then a four-pound Yorkshire terrier puppy, had black wavy fur with brown accents, a face as cute as a stuffed teddy bear, and eyes as blue as the ocean outside our window. But Buddy wasn't just an adorable living souvenir from my fun Miami trip. He became my lifeline and my peace.

There was one peculiarity about Buddy. His face kind of looked like Robert's, including the fact that his blue eyes made me think about the blue that sometimes glinted in Robert's eyes. If Robert and I were on good terms and I looked at Buddy, I would feel warm toward him. But if I was upset with Robert, then Buddy's presence would trigger me. Buddy wanted to comfort and cuddle with me when he sensed that I was in a bad mood, but because Robert was the source of my anger, I didn't want to be bothered and might shoo Buddy away from me. I had to check myself on this a few times.

One day, Buddy ran away. As you might imagine, the logistics of me caring for a dog when I was mostly trapped in a room somewhere could be challenging and required me to use wee-wee pads for Buddy. But if I had run out of them, or if Buddy needed to walk or run around a bit for a little motivation, I would have to let him out of my room, and his needs would have to be addressed by whoever was on the other side of the door, whether that was a runner, a bodyguard, a driver, or Robert's kids' nanny.

Usually after Buddy had his needs attended to, he hung out for a while. Then he'd scratch at my door and I'd let him back in. This time, Buddy didn't return. After two days, I alerted a member of Robert's staff—through an alias—and they confirmed that Buddy was not in the house. Upset, I figured that Buddy must have felt like me. He was tired of being trapped in a room and not living the life of a normal dog who would be walked regularly and who could investigate his environment. So he made a run for it.

I was distraught and needed some assistance. I cracked open my door and whispered, "Help." Judy, the nanny for Robert's kids, who was staying at Olympia Fields during their parental visitation at the time, heard me and came closer. I told her about my crisis. She and I snuck out of the house and drove around the neighborhood looking for him. We didn't find him on the first day, so we went out again the next day. I spotted Buddy's wobbly walk alongside a girl I had never seen before and immediately knew it was him. I was afraid to make a scene, but I wanted my dog back. So I asked her if he was hers. She said she had found him. (Judging from the well-fitting Burberry coat and studded dog collar Buddy was wearing, it looked like she had planned to keep him.) I called Buddy's name, and he ran straight to me. I removed the items and gave them back to her. And I took Buddy with me.

Back at the Olympia Fields house, Robert's runners bought Buddy more wee-wee pads and took him to be shampooed and groomed. Then he disappeared back into the room of the person nobody knew… until the next time.

When Robert's trial began on May 20, 2008, I was living at the Homewood Suites Hotel in Orland Park, about thirty minutes away from Robert's Olympia Fields home. When Robert rode to the courthouse for his trial, sometimes I would travel there on his tour bus with him. While Robert's lawyer, Sam Adam Jr., asked in the courtroom, "Where's the victim? Why isn't she here?" I *was* there in the courthouse parking lot, sitting on the bed in the cubicle-sized bedroom at the back of Robert's tour bus. I didn't have the TV on, of course. Robert wouldn't let me follow the trial, just like he'd forbidden me from watching his televised BET interview with Ed Gordon or listening to his radio interviews since his indictment six years before. I wasn't allowed to watch, listen to, or read anything that could make me question things: not the news or trending social media stories. So, even though I was two hundred feet from Robert, I might as well have been two thousand miles away.

As the trial was unfolding, I knew close to nothing. I did know which of my family members would testify that it was me on the videotape and which ones would side with Team Valerie in the name of defending my honor. But I didn't know much else. I had no idea that everyone in the courtroom watched all twenty-six and a half minutes of that hateful tape, that everyone had seen my immature breasts and watched my face get peed on, had listened to me slur my words while Robert kept refilling my glass with Champagne. I had no way of knowing that Simha, one of my childhood best friends, was asked by Robert's lawyer how she could know it was me by looking at my vagina or that his lawyer would call the girl in the video—me—both a sweet girl and a teen having "raunchy, dirty, nasty sex" during his defense of Robert. I could not know that jurors silently gasped or snickered while a gallery full of spectators did the same as they watched a child pornography video for a trial about child pornography.

It's painful to think about, even now. Horrifying to know that the man who I was lying for didn't give a shit that everyone who could snag a spot in the gallery of Illinois's hottest courtroom drama of the decade could watch as my young, naked, brown body was degraded and abused for free, my first and last name in everyone's mouth. I wonder, if my body hadn't been brown, would anyone outside of the jury have seen it exposed and abused? Would anyone even know my name?

The prosecution, which was litigating a whole case about the exploitation of a little brown girl's body, didn't do anything. The defense, defending Robert from the despicable charges that they knew he was guilty of, didn't say anything. Robert didn't lean over and whisper his concerns to his lawyers. The judge let this happen in his courtroom, unbothered. At the end of his day in court, as Robert filled me in on all the highlights, he didn't tell me any of that. Of course he wouldn't. His team claimed it wasn't him, claimed it wasn't me, argued I wasn't a child.

But it was me. And I was a child. A fourteen-year-old girl who was still a virgin when Robert asked her to name her body parts and their age, and who answered, "Yes, Daddy," when he asked her, "Daddy fuck you?" for the camera. I know that so many people would argue that I have no right to be angry. I wasn't there. I lied. And they would be right about that part. I *wasn't* there. But there were other girls and young women in that gallery, a roomful of people who watched a little girl get violated repeatedly as they replayed portions of the videotape throughout the monthlong trial.

Just for argument's sake, let's imagine I was there, sitting on the witness stand, watching people's eyes dart between my clothed twenty-three-year-old body and the naked fourteen-year-old body on the tape as I testified. Suppose I left the courtroom and by the time I got home there were new blog and vlog posts explaining to all the folks who couldn't make it to court that day whether my current body looked like my child's body and if I was pretty enough for R. Kelly to have gotten himself into such a mess of trouble because of me.

I can't tell you what happened in that trial from my firsthand recollection, I know. I must live with the choices my parents and I made, and with Robert's abuse of other women and girls who met him *after* he was acquitted. That number included an underage Jerhonda Johnson (now Jerhonda Pace), who cut school to support him during the trial and ended up meeting him in front of the courthouse right after he was acquitted. I'm not saying we did the right thing. And I regret that so many more people were hurt by Robert because he wasn't stopped in 2008.

One person who did testify for the prosecution was Lisa Van Allen. Robert told me at the end of her first day of testimony, and I remembered her well. She used to be around frequently when I was fourteen and she was seventeen; Robert liked for us to have threesomes with him. I remembered us being jealous of each other, and that she kept trying to get into my business, like she could tell something wasn't right. I remembered when Robert told me she stole the tape and had a negative motive and vindictive spirit. He told me she was one of the bad people, so I stayed clear of her. The truth is, I don't know what Lisa's motives were. I really don't know her at all. But now I can say that she was brave.

I knew that June 13, 2008, would be the day that Robert was going to find out the verdict. I spent the day bonding with Buddy and talking to God about how grueling my enforced seclusion had been for me. As I prayed, I imagined the verdict would be a burden lifted because my family would no longer have the what-ifs of the trial; everything would be put to rest for us, and we would no longer be bothered by the media or people's opinion. I also prayed that Robert wouldn't go to jail. I was considering his children, his career, how we would look to the public. I just wanted relief.

My phone rang. The phone number was Robert's, so I answered. Robert was crying.

I was silent, my breath shallow.

"Babe, they came out with a verdict."

"Okay." I was nervous. I wasn't watching TV, so I didn't know. "What was it?"

"Not guilty!" he shouted, his voice filled with tears.

I started crying. Tears of joy that this long, draining season was finally over. Relief that I wouldn't feel responsible for him going to jail.

"We did it, baby. We did it!"

It wasn't a long conversation; Robert still had to meet with his lawyers. When we got off the phone, I cried and prayed some more.

So many thoughts were running through my head. It struck me that, on the flip side of him being found not guilty was the fact that our relationship was still a secret. At the time, Robert and Andrea were already separated. (Their divorce would be finalized by January 2009, and Robert had already told his close circle that he was at peace with it because he had been blessed with our love.) I started dreaming about the possibilities and the freedom we could now have within our relationship.

The agony of going through court and having to hide had taken a huge toll on our relationship dynamic. I looked forward to releasing those pressures. I'd be able to be back around my family for holidays. I could let go of all the stress and secrets I'd been shouldering for so many years. I wanted to get my life back, my family, my relationship... and all the things. Now that Robert was acquitted, I wanted to win.

CHAPTER 10

KEPT

> If there is only one thing in my life that I am proud of, it's that I've never been a kept woman.
>
> —Marilyn Monroe

I HAD NEVER GIVEN Marilyn Monroe much thought until this quote credited to her appeared on the screen of my laptop. I stared at it like I didn't know who had put it there. I knew I hadn't. During Robert's trial, he forbade me from looking at the internet or watching the news. I was so used to shielding myself from any and every questionable snippet of information that would interrupt my peace or make Robert mad, that even though the trial was over, and I was allowed to surf the internet more freely, I still tensed up with fear if I saw something Robert might disapprove of. Besides, the list of subjects I was forbidden from doing a Google search on was a mile long. Top five among them:

1. R. Kelly
2. Lisa Van Allen

3. Andrea Kelly
4. Sparkle Edwards
5. Reshona Landfair (multiple spellings)

Marilyn Monroe was not on the list. But as I reread this quote, I felt the hairs on the back of my neck stand on end. If Robert had known she said something like this, he'd probably ban her too. He wouldn't want me to know more about why she said it or to whom. (And if she didn't really say it, he wouldn't want me to know who actually did.) The reason was simple: Even though I had never heard the term *kept woman* before, I was sure I was one.

With the trial over, Robert was back doing his career thing full throttle. He was free to travel with no restrictions, so he was mainly away. For business purposes, he said. But I kept getting calls from folks in Robert's circle about him being sighted out and about at parties and events, or pictures texted to me showing Robert's arms littered with sexy young women I didn't recognize.

I, on the other hand, was not sighted anywhere because he kept me out of sight. As before, I was still staying in the office of his house, miserable. Since he was away most of the time, Robert used a combination of bodyguards in Chicago 24/7 to limit my movements, explaining that he wanted the hubbub following his acquittal to die down. My main job was serving as caregiver for his three kids—who were then about seven, nine, and eleven years old—either in coordination with their primary nanny, Judy, or in place of her if she was unavailable. The irony in that was Robert was still keeping me under his thumb and limiting my access to my own family, but more often than not, when his kids came to Olympia Fields for their court-ordered visitation with him, he wasn't even there. Instead, I was trying to create fun for them and make sure their needs were met.

(Now's a good time for me to explain my decision to mention Robert's now-adult children only minimally in this book. Out of respect for the fact that they were little when so much of what I share here was happening, and that it may trigger lots of complicated feelings for them, I have decided not to share much beyond expressing my love for them. Not only did I babysit the oldest from the time she was tiny and care for all three during their parental visitation, but I also formed a strong bond with Judy, the kids' longtime nanny, whom they love and respect. I realize it can seem strange that this could be so, but the truth is, Judy and I spent lots of time with the kids and each other at the Olympia Fields house. Yes, I was still being hidden from the world and remained a shadowy figure to many, but I was a whole person to Judy and the kids. They were to me, too. Judy was a compassionate and stable presence for the children for many years of their childhood, especially as they adjusted to their parents' separation and divorce. I lost touch with Judy for several years, but we rekindled our friendship during my pregnancy. I am happy to have her as a true godmother to my son.)

These relationships were good for me *despite* Robert, not because of him. (In fact, he fired Judy when he realized that we had a genuine connection and she wasn't spying on me the way he wanted her to when he sent us to run errands for the kids. Thankfully, Andrea recognized how vital Judy was as her children's nanny and hired her directly.) But I was about twenty-four and knew I should have been at least as free as Robert was to live my whole entire life. *I* wasn't the one who had been on trial. Why was I still being kept as a secret? Our relationship was practically nonexistent, so there was no good reason for me to be kept at Olympia Fields. Even Robert's kids would point out the latest pictures of the new women he was dating that were displayed all throughout the living room when they were visiting. And when Robert was in town, I was no longer invited to his studio to watch him create. Instead, he would come into the house and play his new music for me. It was clear he had replaced me with an entirely new circle of women.

Robert's divorce from Andrea had been finalized for five or six months when I found out he was finally going on his much-anticipated trip to Africa. It was one of those rare occasions when he was in Chicago, and we were sitting in the lounge at Robert's Olympia Fields home listening to some of his new music. He was in a good mood, another thing that was becoming rare.

"Do you like it?"

I nodded.

Robert looked at me, his face breaking into an unrehearsed smile of joy.

"What's got you smilin'?" I grinned at him, wanting to share in his pleasure.

"The whole Africa thing is *finally* coming together! I've been tryin' to manifest this for a minute!"

"Wow, Robert." I refused to call him Daddy. I dared him to scold me through my stare. He didn't. "Yeah, I remember." Years before—shortly after he was indicted in 2002—Robert had said he wanted to become an even more internationally famous artist by making music with a more African-, Asian-, and Latin-inspired sound. So, since he was barred from traveling outside of the country due to his legal issues, Robert had the studio decorated to look like a rain forest for inspiration. Now that Robert was free to travel once again, his Africa trip was on.

"Yeah, you know, after all I been through, felt like the right time to go to the Motherland. Soak up some of that African sun. Let them lay hands on me." He smirked. "That's why Black people are all fucked up. We were torn from Africa, you know? How you gonna do that and expect people not to be fucked up?"

I knew he wasn't looking for an answer, so I didn't give one.

"So anyway, what d'you think?"

"About what?" My mind was stewing in Robert's news. It had always been a dream of mine to go to Africa, a dream I had bashfully shared with Robert years before when I was still a teen.

"The music I just played you. You didn't say anything."

Who the hell cares? "I thought I did. It's nice." I forced a smile onto my lips. "I was thinking about the trip to Africa. Your trip. Remember me telling you that was my dream? I'd been to Europe and the Caribbean, but Africa was my dream. It still is." I smiled again.

"Maybe you'll go one day, Sho."

"Can't I go with you?"

"Why you askin' that? You know how things are. I'm going to South Africa and Nigeria as a kind of spiritual journey, you know. A cleansing, I guess. New possibilities and all that. And if I hit good and everything goes well, then maybe I'll sign on the dotted line for a couple of opportunities."

"Okay?"

"And besides, they're planning a big media junket and shit. It's gonna be a whole bunch of meetings. And it's probably gonna be hot as a muthafucka. You don't need to be there for that."

"It gets hot in Chicago." I rolled my eyes. "And I don't have to attend all the press stuff. Or I can wear sunglasses and a wig and stand around with all your fans. But it doesn't matter if they see me. Who cares if they see me? No one has seen me in seven fucking years, Robert! They probably think I'm dead."

"Calm the fuck down, Sho! And don't nobody think you're dead. Look, they puttin' together my spiritual journey to Africa. They know better than me what that needs to look like. So don't start asking me to, like, tack you on to the trip like it's that simple."

"It *is* simple. They work for *you*. It's *your* trip. You can have anyone there you want. And you know it."

"This is why I don't be rockin' with you the same, Sho! You always pickin' a fight when we was just chillin', having a nice evening and shit. How do you expect me to get hard and want to please you and shit when you're in my face making crazy demands?"

"What's crazy? Wanting to leave the house? Wanting to see the light of day? Wanting to experience more than the four walls of this R. Kelly museum with pictures of all the women you've fucked, except me, your best one? What's *crazy* is you expecting me to want to live like this, like I'm a prisoner. I want to go to Africa. With you. God knows I need a spiritual journey!"

Robert sucked his teeth. "I don't need all this mouthing off. Don't make me wanna go nowhere with you. You not like you used to be, Sho."

"Neither are you, Robert."

"Stop calling me that."

"It's your name."

One morning, I woke up and left Robert's house under false pretenses. I told the bodyguard on duty I needed to buy emergency tampons. His grimace let me know he was happy to let me run that errand myself. But what I did was go get some new passport photos taken and then submit a new passport application. I decided that, if I wanted to go to Africa, I needed to be ready if my chance came.

Shortly after Robert's indictment in 2002, when my parents and I met with our Robert-provided lawyers before we lied to the grand jury, they took my passport, among other things. In my passport photo, I was wearing the small silver cross my parents had gotten me for my thirteenth birthday. It was the same cross I had on in the infamous leaked video of Robert and me. I never got that passport back.

Once my new passport arrived in the mail to my parents' address, Dad let me know. I timed my second brief escape for after Mom left to go to her shoe store. If Dad was home, I knew he wasn't going to blow my cover. When I got there, no one was home. I was relieved and heartbroken all at once.

I didn't make it to Africa. Robert was treated like royalty at every stop on his trip. Every move he made was covered in the local, national, and international African press. He was so well received that the following year, Robert returned to South Africa to kick off the 2010 FIFA World Cup singing one of his new songs—backed by the Soweto Spiritual Singers—which became the official anthem of those games.

I was kept on a short leash. Robert could tell that my heart was no longer in our relationship, and he stayed paranoid that I would turn on him. Whenever the mood struck him, he would try to make me take lie detector tests or write crazy letters saying that I was never abused, never held anywhere against my will, and admitting to all kinds of degrading and embarrassing things as still more blackmail.

I didn't have money. He'd give me only enough to do something specific.

I didn't have a bank account. He never allowed me to save money.

I didn't have an education. The last two years of high school had been homeschooling while hiding out. I got decent grades, but I didn't learn much. And following graduation, I wasn't allowed to pursue additional training or a college degree.

I couldn't hold a job. That would give me too much independence.

I had trashed my budding music career years before, and Robert would surely make my name trash in the music industry if I tried to revive it.

Robert was all I had, and I didn't even have him. Not his love. Not his time.

What kept me there were the shreds of pride I had managed to hold on to along with deep feelings of inadequacy. The words that kept ringing in my head were *I'm leaving this situation to go into what?* What was I qualified to do other than please Robert sexually? I had become expert at sex on demand. I had learned to ignore my own discomfort, hurt, and shame to service the man I told myself I loved. I could lie with a straight face and without my heart rate going up.

My peers were passing me by: graduating from college, traveling, starting careers, getting married. I wasn't on track for any of that. I had turned my back so completely on everyone and everything that had once been important to me that I didn't know what I could do other than be Robert's woman in whatever form he dictated.

I tried to tell myself that I was still special in Robert's eyes because he still chose to keep me around. But even that rang false in my own mind. I was always insecure, jealous, and fearful. For a couple more years, I tried to stick things out with this man. If I didn't, I knew I'd look stupid. If I went back to my family, I was positive I'd get a big, fat "I told you so." And after walking Robert's chalk line and telling Robert's lies to avoid public ridicule, if I walked out of my situationship with Robert now, I'd have to deal with the full measure of public humiliation without Robert's help or protection. I'd be this failed person who put Robert on a pedestal for so many years and who gave him everything I had and could hope to be just to be slandered as a stupid ho. No one would remember that I had been a sexually abused child. No one would give a shit that this made me an emotionally stunted woman who didn't feel empowered or even worthy of making my own decisions. *No one would give a shit.* If anything, you'd hurl insults at me. You'd call me a homewrecker… at least many of you did.

How was it that Marilyn Monroe, whose pinup photos men masturbated to in the 1940s, '50s, and '60s, could say she wasn't a kept woman? Maybe she just didn't care what they thought. I wanted not to care.

The first thing that started to change for me was that I stopped being afraid of him.

I was in a rage all the time. Depending on how violent our fights were, Robert would have one of his assistants arrange to get me something, making my self-worth equal to a fancy meal, shopping spree, or piece of jewelry. By 2009, I had reached a breaking point; I couldn't take the abuse anymore. I was a miserable person and couldn't keep living like this. It wasn't even living, just existing. Dark thoughts closed in on me.

I prayed, this time asking God to take the love I had for Robert away from me. I knew that this relationship was more bad than good, and I was mourning the loss of having meaningful connections with everyone who had been important to me.

Robert didn't know how to handle me. I grabbed the reins and snatched them out of his hands, started doing things out of character to make him not like me. I dressed seductively to draw the attention of other men. I became a flirt, which he had expressly forbidden.

Robert started to see the writing on the wall. I had no more to give him. I would not. I had become a liability. At my insistence, he gave me money to get an apartment. He started letting me go look for jobs. Then he phased me out of his living arrangements.

I was twenty-six when I officially left Robert. But though I was gone from his home, I wasn't free. My mind was messed up. I knew I had deficits. It was those deficits that kept me bound to him. I needed his money to pay my rent. Now that I was living on my own and forced to make decisions for myself, I realized just how bad I was at it. Every day that Robert didn't tell me who I was to him, I stared in the mirror and saw all that I wasn't. At twenty-six, I had managed to finally leave, but I was afraid of the wreck the rest of my life would be without him.

I looked the part. I couldn't afford to even get my hair done. The circle of people I could confide in was only one person big—Robert. I had learned to depend on him for everything, even my own thoughts! It was hard learning how to be a woman in the world at twenty-six.

"Alyssa." I spoke the name of my old friend into the phone. One of my few bright spots when I was under Robert's thumb, our friendship had managed to outlast our shared connection to Robert. I told her a little bit about how things with Robert came to a miserable end. She didn't want to hear it all. I was too ashamed to tell her anyway. She became a kind of peer mentor for me. Alyssa was a hairstylist by profession. So even though I didn't have any money, Alyssa did my hair.

PART THREE

I GOTTA FIND PEACE OF MIND

Please come free my mind.
Please come meet my mind.
Can you see my mind?

—Lauryn Hill

CHAPTER 11

HARM REDUCTION

THE LAST DAY OF my twenties already felt like a distant memory. Waking up to my new decade under the crisp white sheets of my hotel bed and with the Caribbean Sea outside the room's floor-to-ceiling window glistening under the early-morning sunlight felt like God's will for my life. I stan for Chicago any day, but this right here...

Jamaica. I had wanted to gift something to myself to mark this birthday. For as long as I could remember, my big birthdays had been planned or financed by Robert. This trip was low-key but *I* had made it happen for myself. Long before Beyonce sang "Break My Soul" and her Renaissance world tour, I felt like I was having my own personal renaissance. Choosing to book this trip felt liberating, like I was claiming my own womanhood. Here I was, the authentic Reshona I was becoming without having to slide my eyes over at someone else for approval. Maybe this was healing.

Life was looking up. It was 2014. I had my own job and apartment. I was rekindling friendships, making new ones, and happy not to have a man. I didn't want anyone to look for *anything* from me. This new decade was going to be free of all the things that had weighed me down for so many years of my twenties and teens. I didn't know what to expect or what I wanted, but I was excited not to be where I had been.

The sun washed my sheets—and my coworker and travel buddy's sleeping frame—in the gold light of early morning. I looked over as she stirred on her bed. "Hey, birthday woman," she murmured.

"Hey." I smiled into the sun, letting it bathe me in warmth.

"I know it's your birthday and all, but we still trying to sleep over here!"

Chuckling quietly, I whispered, "I know." It was too early to get dressed and go down for breakfast. But it wasn't too early to feel gratitude. In my heart, I was privately celebrating things she didn't know about me and therefore couldn't understand. The gift of choosing where I wanted to be in the world and how I wanted to show up. The free will to express my own thoughts and make my own decisions.

She didn't know my past, and that was okay. We weren't close friends, but in some ways, that was a gift, too. I enjoyed trying on this thirty-year-old Reshona who wasn't bound to what everyone thought they knew about her. It felt like a glimpse of freedom that I hoped would grow in this new decade of mine.

I closed the curtains to darken the room, but the sun continued to rise within me as I lay there imagining a future that seemed so undiscovered. My post-traumatic stress still made me a little scared to make too many plans.

I was hopeful.

Hope springs eternal. The future is bright. Every corny phrase pops into your head, but they feel exactly right. You latch on to them, revel in them. The future belongs to you too. You're amazed by this.

The burdens of your last decade are receding farther into the past as you step across the threshold into something new.

Would this be my year of yes?

What was it about being on vacation that makes you think the path forward will be straight and uncomplicated? All about manifesting your dreams? But returning to the Chi woke me up. Quickly. Don't get me wrong: My hometown is flowing with as much milk and honey as anyplace, but when I returned, I realized three things:

1. I didn't have just a future here; I had a history, too.
2. The internet was a pain in my God-given behind.
3. My peers had been adulting for a minute and I was in catch-up mode.

Possibility? True. Hope? Check. But I was a Landfair, and in Chicago, that meant a few things. I wasn't alone, for one. That was mostly a good thing. I still had more cousins than I could shake a stick at. People knew my dad as a great musician, and increasingly, my brother too. Folks had worked with my cousins or had attended the church my Grandpa Bo pastored. Grandma Ruby, as the genteel first lady, always had a bake sale in support of someone's special cause. It meant something to be a Landfair in Chicago.

Being Reshona Landfair, however, had another whole set of associations. Since my name was not redacted during Robert's 2008 trial, that meant my first and last names were in everybody's mouth, both in the courtroom and out. And because Sparkle wouldn't stop talking about me in practically every interview she did for morning talk shows, radio shows, and whatever else, folks just wouldn't forget Reshona Landfair. The only minor saving grace was that people didn't know how to spell my name.

I mostly disregarded all that noise. During my time with Robert, I became accustomed to ignoring the media. Even though I was now free to consume it, I was very selective about what I watched and read. Nevertheless, the DMs that kept finding me on social media let me know that although I was trying to mind my business and keep it positive, there was a whole corner of the internet full of amateur media personalities who built their following talking about Robert, my family, and me. (There's also plenty about Robert's abuse of Aaliyah and other girls and women.)

This was exhausting for me. Here I was, a thirty-something grown woman working hard at being whole and healthy, but at any given moment—whether out with friends or enjoying a night of left-over Giordano's deep-dish pizza and scrolling on my phone—folks who recognized me would make nasty accusations about "my kind" or launch flaming arrows at me over the socials. When I was out with friends, I probably was convincing when my quick wit kicked in with a biting comeback or I rolled my eyes and shrugged the attacks off with an insincere "God bless you, too!" Then I'd ignore the stares of folks around me and go back to whatever we were doing because I didn't want to make my friends feel uncomfortable. The truth was it hurt. Using my extroverted personality as a shell, I buried the pain and kept it moving. Most days, I just wanted to fly below the radar. Being unknown or wrapping myself in my protective shell, however, was a kind of punishment. I didn't realize it then, but I was starving for meaningful connections where I would be known and loved for being uniquely myself.

This was why I loved the opportunity to connect with my family.

Before Robert constrained my movements, I had free rein with them: visiting them, playing with my cousins at the park or laughing (quietly) with them in church, and even eating dinner with them without asking my mom for permission beforehand.

As a woman reclaiming my life, I was eager to catch up with everyone: to meet spouses and babies, see apartments and houses, congratulate them belatedly on life accomplishments. Most times, my family received me well. But sometimes the interactions were awkward for me, highlighting how out of step my life was with most of my peers' and leaving me feeling ignorant about the most basic things.

Sparkle's fiftieth birthday was coming. It was hard to believe for so many reasons, not least of which was how many of the years between her twenty-fifth and fiftieth we had been estranged. The momentous occasion would give me a chance to be around folks who knew me before I became that foolish girl, before I was a secret or a punch line. No, everything was not all good in the hood with me and each of my family members, but the passage of time had dulled some of the jagged edges that had once been so pronounced. Ironically, the fact that I was *invited* to Sparkle's party told me how things had changed with my family, for better and worse. Better because I was invited and could choose to attend. And worse because when our family used to throw family parties, you never needed an invitation. If it was happening, then you just showed up!

Sparkle was the belle of her own ball. I knew that her party probably wasn't going to be the moment for any big heart-to-hearts with her, but our quick catch-up did include her asking me if I was still keeping up with folks at the studio since *Buzzfeed* published some wild article about an R. Kelly cult and the #MuteRKelly movement was gaining steam. She also wondered if I would consider doing interviews, so I thought she might create some space for deeper conversation. Maybe she felt she had, and that my throwaway answer of "I'm good" said everything she needed to know.

My beautiful Aunt Sparkle.

Somewhere inside of me, I want you to ask about me, to *really* ask if I'm okay, beyond our new normal of gossip-tinged superficial exchange. Don't get me wrong: I'm happy that we're cool with each other and enjoy when we share a kiki or party together since our friend circles overlap. But for all the fun and chitchat, whenever we have a moment to speak directly, I leave those conversations feeling like you're fishing for intel and trying to keep both sides of your bread buttered in relation to Robert.

Your party is a celebration of your milestone, of who you have become, but as much as I try not to think about the past, I keep growing nostalgic for when you called me Chon and you referred to me as your heart. Don't you want to check in with your heart?

Maybe the questions feel too hard to answer. But I only have one: *Why?* You knew what I didn't: that Robert was a messy serial adulterer at best. Of course, you knew him since 1989 and began working with him in 1992. But even if you thought that 1994 Aaliyah marriage rumor was a hoax, I was seventeen when you told journalist Jim DeRogatis that Robert's "whole MO" was grooming "ripe and young" girls.[2]

Maybe the answer to my question forces you to confront your own difficult experiences when you were a young woman trying to make it. Did you tell yourself that you were preparing me for the sexual pay to play you knew firsthand to be an ugly aspect of the business I wanted to be a part of? Or maybe you thought I could do a lot worse than to be connected to *the R. Kelly*, even if that meant I had to give him my virginity. After all, I wouldn't be the first girl to have to pay a powerful man with my body and silence.

Maybe you thought that because you were Robert's protégée and lover, you'd be able to protect me from his worst instincts, or that making me a member of his family, so to speak, would help him to see me differently and leave me alone.

As we celebrate your fiftieth birthday, I realize that we are both more than twenty years removed from the decisions you made that changed the trajectory of our lives. If you could climb back into your twenty-something head and explain your thoughts and motivations, I bet neither of us would be satisfied with your answers. But I'm not looking for the right answers, Sparkle. Many decisions made on my behalf were wrong. I just want you to push past what's uncomfortable and speak to your "heart," woman to woman.

The pageantry of Sparkle's glitterati guest list was legendary, rivaling any runway.

I watched her as she greeted them—the Black and beautiful of our beloved Chi-town and plenty more who'd flown in from the coasts because they couldn't miss the party of the year—and pushed my lips into a smile. The few minutes of conversation we had managed to grab still jangled around my head.

"Mr. R. is still the biggest dog in the dog pound." Sparkle rolled her eyes.

"Yeah." I was noncommittal.

"You keep up with him, right?"

I nodded.

"Well, I'm still out here making music. That's what I do. So maybe I'll work with him again. I mean, I'm open. The devil you know and all that jazz." She took a sip of her mocktail.

I raised my eyebrow. I thought she hated him for what he did to me and to her. But then I remembered what she had told me the last time we chatted: She and her boyfriend were trying to get a reality show off the ground and wanted to know if I wanted in. "I'd like to say I'm surprised," I answered finally.

"Sounds like you're throwing shade." She stared at me.

"I'm not." I was. Her contradictions made me feel skeptical. Maybe I seemed contradictory to her, too. After all, I said Robert and I were cool, when she and I both knew he didn't deserve any of my friendship. The difference, I guess, was that she seemed to be looking for opportunities while I was just trying to live my life. It made me sad that we both felt like we needed to carve out new lanes for ourselves in our home city because Robert still had enough influence in Chicago to put his thumb on every scale. Whether it was Sparkle navigating her music career or me seeking a relationship with someone who wouldn't see me as a curiosity or source of bragging rights, we kept bumping into Robert's skeletons.

Nevertheless, the party was fun. Sparkle looked fabulous, and everyone was in high spirits. It was as if I finally had the big sister/girlfriend in Sparkle that I was always supposed to have and that Robert squashed. In that moment, all the old bad feelings of competition, skepticism, and jealousy melted away. I was embraced by Sparkle and her friends like a long-lost little sister. The evening full of double-kisses on the cheek and good ole Chicago steppin', it felt great to have this piece of family fun again—even in a frivolous and temporary way—and I was happy to no longer be the reason for broken relationships within my family. And since I was a full-fledged adult, I wasn't excluded from the libations and hilarity that followed.

* * *

It was the day after Christmas. I was feeling lazy, and since I didn't have anywhere I had to be, I decided to hang on to the bed until sometime past noon. Rubbing sleep from my eyes, I looked at my phone and saw I had fifteen text messages from ten different people. What the hell? Why were folks blowing up my phone?

> Girl, WYA?
> Shon, turn on Lifetime TV.
> Hope you sittin' down!

I was afraid of what I was going to see. Folks saw Sparkle boo-hooing on a commercial for a new show called *Surviving R. Kelly*. I had been hearing some whispers about this show for the past couple weeks, but my old training to keep far away from any media related to Robert kicked in, and I tried to put it out of my mind as something that was far from me. But knowing that Sparkle was connected to it made my stomach clench up. I clicked on the TV and waited. It didn't take too long before I saw what others already had. What in the actual hell! *Didn't I just see Sparkle at Granny's homegoing services in October and her birthday party in May? Hadn't we caught up?* Or so I thought. There was no way on God's green earth that she didn't know she was going to do this show when I saw her in May. And by October, she *had* to know this show was going to come out at the top of the new year. I was shook.

I had thought this shit was over. I was trying to keep my name out of folks' mouths if I could. And now this! How was it that this situation was resurfacing again and Sparkle didn't even have the decency to give me a heads-up? I mean, she and I were back cool, right? We had each other's numbers and everything. We had even cried together as a family as Granny grew weaker and passed away from Alzheimer's just a couple months before.

Now, as our family was healing—as *I* was healing—I was slapped in the face by Sparkle crying about *my* abuse on some Lifetime docuseries. I felt nauseous just trying to imagine what this all meant. If Sparkle could cry on TV *about* me, then it seemed that she could have shed some of those tears *with* me. She didn't have to let me find out on TV that the worst experience of my life was going to be the topic of a multipart television series. Sparkle's not a monster and I know she loves me, but I couldn't understand why she was being cagey and doing the same tired stuff: talking for me and about me to other people without bothering to talk to me! Sparkle kept deputizing herself to tell folks my story. But it wasn't my story. It was a version of *hers*.

My mind was going a mile a minute. I was trying to figure out what I needed to know, what I needed to do. I didn't know what the hell would come out through the Lifetime show, so I tried to prepare myself. Only God knew who else would be involved to tell whatever they thought they knew about me. I reflected on the title of the show and the other folks I saw on the commercials. I knew at least half of them! And the other half... They must have been there to talk about something other than me. I had thought that I was the only one who had been gullible, who he had tried to break. But I wasn't even on the show. It was beginning to dawn on me that this story of "surviving" Robert was bigger than me, bigger than I could have imagined.

I needed more information about the show, but I couldn't figure out who to call. I was too angry at Sparkle, and I wasn't ready to hear her lame-ass excuses. I would have to tell my parents, and break it to them as gently as possible that the show might cover some of the terrible stuff I had been part of. Although they had lied to cover up my illicit relationship with Robert right along with me, I hadn't explained the dehumanizing acts Robert forced upon me. The trailer of the show let me know that some of that shit was about to come out in a major way. I had to get to my parents before the show did.

But first, I needed to know more.

I reached out to Robert and his manager and accountant, Derrel McDavid. I know what you're thinking: *WTF.*

I was still in a place of such neediness that I reached out to my abuser for help, but that was lost on me then; I was acting from a place that felt familiar. I didn't let myself think that deeply about it. I rationalized that he would know more than anyone else about the show. We were on cordial speaking terms. I texted back and forth with him a few times before and during the airing of *Surviving R. Kelly.* I got short responses or no response at all. Robert wasn't much of a writer, remember. He preferred to call.

When Robert and I did speak, I was jittery and wanted reassurance. "Do I have anything to worry about?" I asked.

Robert laughed off my question. "R. Kelly's got haters, Sho. That shit ain't nothin' new." He snickered again. "But for real, though, I don't know jack shit about that show."

"You don't." I side-eyed him through the phone.

"Look, I don't know what you want me to tell you. You acting like I put the show together. I mean, go ask Lifetime. Go ask Sparkle! Didn't you say she's in it? I don't know why you asking me." Robert sniffed.

I listened to his nonsense for a few more minutes before realizing the call was a waste of time, and I abruptly ended it.

Derrel was equally tight-lipped. But he did have a message that he repeated: "Don't hurt him. Don't hurt Robert. I know there were a lot of things that happened that, you know, shouldn't have or that could have been avoided. But don't hurt him."

Derrel's message surprised me because, at the time, I didn't know what he did. Not only were Derrel and Robert on the outs, but in just a couple months' time, federal charges would be brought against him and June Brown in addition to Robert, and they would end up being on trial together. (Derrel and June were ultimately acquitted.)

As I scanned the names in my phone, I finally landed on one person who had some intelligence that she was willing to share: Diana Copeland. Diana had once worked as an assistant for Robert years before. She was short on specifics, but she was crystal clear about a couple of things. Yes, the Lifetime show was only the beginning of a whole dumpster fire named Robert Kelly. Lots of the people who had been around Robert had lost respect for him—including her—and were no longer working for him, she said. Finding a sympathetic ear in her, I vented about my concerns. She said she knew what I had gone through, and that Robert had lots of people against him. So many, in fact, that things were not looking good for him. I didn't know exactly what that meant, but I knew it meant something big. She mentioned the upcoming Lifetime docuseries and assured me that it didn't mention me by name. But whatever was afoot was more significant than even the docuseries.

Still, facing my parents was going to be even harder. The show was going to air in the first week of January. As you might imagine, this was as awkward as it was painful. I didn't want to say more than I needed to, but since I didn't know exactly what to expect, I had to prep them for the possibility of hearing about more videotapes, threesomes, perverted sex acts, and the fact that Robert peeing on me wasn't a one-off. I was so afraid to relive it, so I just tried to introduce all of this to them without saying too much. Mom and Dad both looked like they had seen a ghost. I knew all too well that it was real, but I agreed that we were being haunted.

I wish this wasn't true, but the day *Surviving R. Kelly* first began airing, I texted Robert. Falling into old habits, I wanted him to reassure me again that my world wasn't about to explode. I also went out with my cousins rather than watch it. I was scared that I'd have a meltdown if I tuned in. But the next day, folks were talking about it and the talk just didn't stop.

I forced myself to watch it. It churned up so many emotions for me. I didn't appreciate Sparkle's appearance "on my behalf." I doubt that I would have agreed to be a part of it myself, but I didn't need an unappointed spokesperson. But more than my annoyance at her, I was floored by all that I heard. Yes, I knew that Robert had other women besides me, but I had no idea how many, how poorly he treated the others, or that there were so many underage girls, lawsuits settled out of court, and nondisclosure agreements. Hearing that opened my eyes to just how calculating, manipulative, and diabolical Robert could be. As someone on the show said, there was a difference between R. Kelly and Robert. It hurt my heart to see how many women knew that terrible difference.

I thought about what Diana alluded to in our conversation: This Lifetime show, as bad as it was, would be just the tip of the iceberg. It was. Not only had the show triggered a new wave of rumors, social media attacks, and phone calls from former friends for me, but by the first week of March 2019, Robert had been hit with dozens of additional accusations, multiple state and federal counts of sexual abuse, and even a couple of arrests.

In the midst of all of that, I got a premonition: Shit was about to get real again, for me and for my parents. But whatever that was going to look like, this time, the outcome had to be different. Deep in the center of my spirit, it felt like God ignited a fire of conviction inside of me to stand up for the truth. Yes, it was going to be scary. So, do it scared, Shon! I had been scared when Robert abused and filmed my body, scared when I retold his lies and hid in whatever room he put me in. What had that gotten me? It sure as hell wasn't the peace or closure I expected. It was just the opposite: a burden. With every job I applied for, friend I made, and date I went on, I was always plagued with worry. Did they know? Would they judge me? I was tired of living in the shadow of Robert's secret that had become mine. I had to purge.

But the purge wouldn't be just for me. I knew that my silence had kept Robert from paying the price for his abuse following his 2008 trial. Free, Robert took the opportunity to pounce on new prey, folks who could have been spared. Hiding in my fear wasn't the answer. Not for me. Not for others. I could not be on the wrong side of history twice.

Empowered by the revelation that I didn't have to feel the way I was trained to feel and could think and act for myself, I felt like I was in preparation mode. I wasn't just Robert's victim. I was a *survivor*, a whole damn woman who was stronger than I realized. And since God was all about justice, he'd be with me, even though I felt like David to Robert's Goliath.

Shortly after that, federal agents from Homeland Security came to my family's home to serve me a subpoena. I wasn't there to receive it. But now my parents and I had an inkling of what was up. I knew what I was going to do and what I'd no longer do. And no, I didn't need permission.

Things were tense at home, a silent standoff with our resurfacing secret that was the elephant in the middle of our living room. We'd wake up, go through the motions of our day, and go to bed in a kind of limbo, as if we were all holding our breath and waiting for what we knew was coming. One day, I woke up sweating, the fire from the other day reignited within me. I surrendered to it. Whatever it wanted me to do, I would do. Walking to the living room, I saw Dad straightening up, the morning sun highlighting his furrowed brow and clenched jaw. Dad's worries were written into his body's every nonverbal cue. Mom was in the kitchen, the clanging of pans and sizzling of bacon and eggs the only sounds. I called a family meeting.

Dad dropped onto a bench and teetered there. Mom rushed in, drying her hands on her housecoat, and sat on Dad's favorite chair. I stood.

Taking a gulp of water from an unclaimed cup on the coffee table, I bounced my gaze between my parents. They looked smaller to me somehow. Not physically, but emotionally. They didn't feel the empowerment I did. "Mom and Dad, if anything comes back around to me, legally I mean, I'm not lying like we did before. Why should I? What has that gotten me or any of us? All he does is just rack up more victims."

Dad looked defeated. "Yeah, well, I don't understand how he still has the audacity to continue this same behavior after he got away with it the first time."

Mom was spooked. "What makes you think that Robert won't do what he threatened to do the first time?"

I shook my head. "I don't think anything, Mom. I don't know what he'll try to do. But I can't keep lying for him. While he's busy avoiding prison, I'm in a prison of his lies. I can't do that again. So, whatever happens, I'm not the one." My eyes were pleading but my tone was firm. "I know I begged you to lie for Robert and me when I was young and thought he loved me. Maybe he did think he loved me in a twisted way, but it really doesn't matter. I'm not the confused and lovesick girl I was. I'm older now and making my own decisions with my eyes wide open. So, please don't lie and call yourself protecting me, or you'll get caught out there alone."

Dad's body folded in on itself like a discarded napkin. He released the breath he'd been holding for days. Nodding in weariness and agreement, his face had lost all its creases.

"Besides," I added, "it looks like lots of folks have turned on him. But even if they hadn't..." My voice trailed off. I was exhausted, like I'd aged a thousand years in the time it took to dredge up the memories I had tried hard to bury somewhere so deep inside of me that they would die without ever seeing the light of day.

"I'm just saying, Reshona, we don't have money and powerful lawyers behind us." Mom's fear was written all over her face.

"But we have the truth."

I was driving down Harlem Avenue in our Oak Park neighborhood with Mom in the passenger seat when I noticed a car behind me. I hadn't been tracking it exactly, but somewhere in my mind I realized the car had been trailing me for at least three blocks. Mom and I were running errands and had just driven past the hotel where Robert first broke the news to Dad that he and I were in a secret relationship. An unmarked detective car pulled alongside our car and directed me to the parking lot of the Wendy's at the corner. A man and a woman in street clothes got out and approached my window. I rolled it down. The crisp air of that early spring day blew through me like the breath of the Holy Spirit. I knew this was the moment my intuition had prepared me for. "Reshona Landfair." The man closest to me said my name as a statement and not a question. He knew he had me, and if I lied, he'd expose it. Quickly.

"Yes?"

"Who are you? You don't just cut a woman off and then demand her name!" Mom raised her voice enough to make it clear she didn't like his presumptuousness.

I turned and looked at her. "No, Mom. This is not that anymore. Calm down." My voice was low, my expression reminding her of our recent conversation. We weren't taking the old approach. We weren't lying.

"I'm from Homeland Security. We're here to issue a subpoena to your daughter, Mrs. Landfair. You'll receive your subpoena later."

Mom sank back into the passenger seat. They knew who she was, too.

"Okay," I answered. "Whatever you need from us, we're cooperating. You can serve me." I marveled at how steady my voice was, how sure I sounded, because inside I felt nervous. Mom's energy was as feisty as it was scared. I was afraid too—we didn't have a lawyer or any backup—but I knew there was nothing else to do but cooperate with the federal government.

As we drove back to my parents' home, I reiterated to Mom that our old approach was buried, so she needed to come out of denial and face this situation, and *not* on Robert's side. When we got home, we debriefed Dad. "Look, I have nothing left in me to continue to lie. So, whatever that looks like on our end, I'm giving you the heads-up that the levies are going to break at this point. I'm letting it all air out. I never want to have to relive this situation again. And the reason why I feel like I'm reliving it right now at this very moment is because I lied to begin with. So I am going to purge my truth, whatever that looks like. Because I can't see myself going through this situation another ten years from now, trying to cover up the truth."

Dad reached out his hand to me and I grabbed it. "Whatever you decide, Reshona, I'm completely with you. I'm also tired. I take accountability. I know it's partly my fault that this happened. It is what it is at this point." He smiled a weak smile, his weariness crushing him into the floor. "I'm with you. I agree with you and I'm standing with you." He knew that whatever consequences came with the truth, it was the lighter load.

Mom pressed her lips together, her energy sending a different message. I watched as she tried to gain control of her twitching face, her right eyelid jumping from nervousness. She squinted in fear at what I imagined was Robert dancing like a boogeyman in her mind's eye. Her body slouched, Mom twisted her wedding ring frantically around her finger. I studied the sunspots on her cheeks, her faraway expression. She was the mother I knew and the woman I didn't completely understand. My eyes got glassy. I don't think she was against the idea of telling the truth; she was still so intimidated by Robert that what was right was in a tug-of-war with what she thought was possible.

My meetings with the federal prosecutors began. Though I had agreed to cooperate, I was conflicted. In my mind, I wanted to tell the whole entire truth, but my body convulsed with so much shame and regret that it was hard to answer. I wanted to vanish. I was amazed and horrified that they expected me to answer questions about and admit to stuff so private, embarrassing, specific, and despicable that I had planned to take all that shit with me to my deathbed. But there I was, sworn to tell the truth, the whole truth, and nothing but the truth, so help me God, and sitting around a table with four people I had never met. I took so many deep breaths that I filled my stomach with air.

They spoke to me with kindness, expressed understanding that these would be hard and invasive questions. I felt supported and protected, like I had some sort of cushion. This was new to me, a complete 180 from the first time I had been deposed for a case against Robert. Then, I had been a teenager flanked by my parents and the lawyer Robert had handpicked for us. We were not cooperating, and our lawyer was what they called combative. I remember thinking that the prosecution's attorneys were the ones who were combative. As I remember it, it felt like they lacked sympathy for the challenging position I was in. But as I reflected on that first experience, I realized that my thoughts about it—just like my thoughts about everything—were filtered through what Robert told me and my mistaken belief that we were on the same side.

I did what I realized I didn't do enough of: I prayed for courage and an obedient spirit. I knew that God didn't want me to lie again. Lying wouldn't be easier, even if it seemed like it would be. This time, even though I was scared and nervous, I didn't feel intimidated. I was a grown woman of nearly thirty-five when our sessions began. I was there without my parents but with a lawyer who represented *me* and not Robert. (Fred, my cousin by marriage who worked in the entertainment industry and who had been supporting me initially, helped me to find a competent and compassionate lawyer with whom I felt comfortable.) Because I knew in my heart that I wanted to be completely truthful and hold nothing back, my oath before God and everyone in that room felt heavy. In those excruciating sessions that ran for three or four hours at a stretch over months and months, I laid everything out on the table. I was trying to clear up every lie I had ever told and clear out every hole I dug for those lies, recognizing that however deep I buried them, that was how far down I had to crawl to bring them out. As I spoke, I was super focused on not perjuring myself. I also thought about how the workers at Robert's studio who seemed to care about me might get hurt. But I had a revelation. Even those people who treated me with kindness still prioritized their paychecks over my humanity. Looking at the federal prosecution's video recorder over and over, I reassured myself that it wasn't there to make videos of me that they would use as blackmail. Then I kept telling the truth.

CHAPTER 12

TREMORS

HAVING MY PERIOD COME late wasn't uncommon. *Stress*, I figured. So much of my world was operating at full tilt. I was still going to the federal courthouse for in-depth sworn depositions at least a couple of times a month. I was living with my parents, holding down a job, and trying to have a grown-up and healthy relationship with a man. The job was fine, and the interviews had become something of a cathartic outlet. I was learning just how much toxic and shameful shit I needed to purge. My relationship was something of a social experiment. I was trying to be in a healthy relationship minus the trauma and manipulation I was used to. It must have been a bizarre experience to have me as a girlfriend. My expectations were always too much or too little.

I was thirty-five when I learned that I was pregnant.

I can't say that I thought our relationship was ready for the introduction of a new little person, but the prospect of becoming a mother felt like a rebirth of hope within me, something I had lost so many years before. And my parents were excited. They saw it as a kind of do-over, an opportunity to be the older and wiser grandparents—qualities they had sometimes lacked when raising me. Lil Greg was no longer little, a twenty-something sought-after drummer who traveled everywhere and was living his best life. He looked forward to being Uncle lil Greg and promised to be the coolest uncle this little boo-boo could ever hope to have.

My then boyfriend's feelings were muted. He was clear that we weren't solid as a couple, so, now that the stakes had suddenly become crazy high, he wondered if we had what it would take to go the distance. He was right to have those concerns; we didn't have what we needed. Out of respect for his privacy, I won't share anything specific about him. But I'll give this backstory: You remember how during the pandemic some people moved in with their girlfriend or boyfriend while others ran in the opposite direction? Folks were forced to evaluate their relationships—whether new loves or twenty-year marriages—with a kind of precision and insight that is almost never required under normal circumstances. Well, I was about four months pregnant when this whole country went on lockdown. My meetings with the feds came to a screeching halt and I lost my job. I was eating for two, and suddenly my family had to figure out how to get groceries delivered to our home. My parents' quarantine bubble became a magnifying glass for the shortcomings of our partnership. August 2020 was in our sights, the month we anticipated becoming parents to our shared human. I think it's safe to say that lockdown likely made my boyfriend realize that even though he had been on the scene when our son was conceived, he hadn't really thought through what it meant for us to be recurring characters in each other's life story.

I wanted our baby more than I wanted our relationship. That's not to say I didn't try; I did. But I realized two things about myself when I was pregnant. The first was that I was more needy than I thought I was, and I didn't know how to feel about that. I had gotten good at handling my business and putting on a brave face to the world. And even when I was purging my experience of abuse to the feds in our sessions, I kept that stuff compartmentalized, tucked into a box that I opened only when I was talking on the record in that conference room. Otherwise, I tried to project that I had my shit on lock.

Unfortunately for me, being in a relationship required vulnerability and openness. But I still thought that being vulnerable meant being foolish, naive, weak, or scared. When I added in the pregnancy wild card and all the changes it brought—physical changes, obviously, and the hormonal rushes of intense emotions—it was a bridge too far. I did better accepting help and support from my parents than from my boyfriend. It was easier to lean on them rather than do the hard work of opening myself up in all these ways to a man who still had an unproven track record. I didn't know how to express my needs because I still struggled with identifying them.

On top of that, my mind was playing tricks on me, making me compare him to a version of Robert that never existed. For example, I imagined that Robert would have been able to predict what I needed and when, that he would have been more attentive. Of course, that wasn't true. Not only had I witnessed Robert being an inept father to the three children he did have, but what I was misremembering as attention toward me was just Robert micromanaging and manipulating me so much that I thought he was anticipating my needs because he brainwashed me into thinking that. That's jacked up, but my mind wasn't as free of Robert's long-term damage as I thought.

The second thing I realized was that becoming a mother would be my shot at redemption. Having a child meant I'd finally get top billing to do something no one else could. I had been chosen by God to shepherd this particular life into the world. And even though the world was screwed up, it would be made better by my child joining it. But this amazing awareness didn't bring out my inner earth mother. It manifested as full-blown anxiety. Everything felt *huge*: the blessing of a new little person and my big aspirations along with the realization that I would coparent with a man who would never be my life partner. By the time our son was born, our relationship was over.

But he was here, healthy and strong! I wanted to embrace my motherhood journey with everything I had. God knows, I was ready to say a permanent goodbye to so much of what had dictated my teens and early adult years and to write a brand-new chapter in my story as I helped my son start his own brand-new book. I wanted to be a good mother and pour my unconditional love into another human. My life had taught me not to be enamored with or intimidated by celebrities, rich people, or flashy things, not to act in fear but to walk in faith, and that you don't have to stay wedded to bad decisions. So with humility, I set upon the journey of pouring into him every good thing Mom and Dad had ever poured into me with greater wisdom and less fear.

But that wasn't how it went. Within days of my newborn son and me being discharged from the hospital, I was readmitted. I had preeclampsia, a serious pregnancy complication that sent my blood pressure through the roof and jeopardized my life. My parents took care of my son at their home while also tending to me as I recovered in the hospital. I'm grateful to God for their loving care and my recovery. Unfortunately, the trauma of pregnancy and new motherhood didn't just affect my body; it also impacted my mind. I had postpartum depression. It would last for nearly two years, forcing my son and me to spend more time at my parents' house than at my new apartment.

It was also why I had to find a new home for my dog, Buddy. Saying goodbye to my companion of twelve years was rough, but as I tackled my new set of challenges, I knew I had to release Buddy from serving as a daily reminder of my past trauma.

Many women who have walked this postpartum depression journey know how debilitating and shameful it can feel. I felt paralyzed, scared that I would fail at the one job that was uniquely mine. All the seeds of fear and inadequacy that Robert had planted in me more than twenty years before were sprouting new leaves and growing deeper roots. Yes, I was doing a good job of dredging up all my trauma and abuse from my former life for the federal prosecutors as they mounted their case against Robert, but I was doing a miserable job of being present and owning the life I was currently living, a life that included being a mother to a baby who didn't ask for my trauma.

My parents didn't miss a beat. I remember when Dad left a show early because of my SOS call to Mom.

"Mom, I don't know how I feel, I don't know what I'm experiencing." I was speaking like a zombie on the phone. I didn't even recognize my own voice.

"That's all right, baby. Your dad will be there soon. I texted him. He's not too far from you. Let's just stay on the phone till he gets there. Then you can come over here so we can help you and monitor you."

When Dad arrived, he packed up my four-month-old baby and me.

Sometimes when I looked at my son, I'd feel overwhelmed. Yes, I loved him. But I felt so many things in addition to love. My heart felt like either an icebox or a raging and uncontained fire. I just didn't know what I had signed up for. Mom would come and sit with me so I could nap, take a bath, or just cry. Both she and my dad encouraged me to get professional support as well. Their love, prayers, and hands-on support, combined with medical support in the form of therapy with a licensed psychologist and a limited course of antidepressant medication, got me through those years.

I watched Dad place his sleeping grandson in his crib. Even though I insisted that my son, at nearly eight months, was too old to be rocked to sleep, Dad said that when grandparents did it, it didn't count. Every day that my son and I were over at my parents'—which was most days of the week when he was a baby—Dad let him sleep in the center of his chest, his little legs making an arc around Dad's ample belly. They both seemed so content that I never had the heart to stop them from their ritual.

"Let's go in the other room," Dad directed.

I followed him to the living room. It was midday and the house was quiet since Mom was at the mall and Dad's pint-sized buddy was asleep. Dad took his usual seat on the recliner. I curled up on the couch.

"I'm proud of you, Reshona." He made the slightest smile, but his tone was serious. "You're a good mom. I know it's been really hard with the postpartum depression and everything you're dealing with. But you're doing it. Facing it. You're a brave woman."

"Thanks, Dad." His words made my heart big. I felt like many things, but not those things. Nevertheless, I received his affirmation because I aspired to grow into it.

"I've tried to be a good person, but sometimes I missed the mark by a marathon mile." Dad paused and thought. "And I'm still working on my bravery. I'm trying to follow in your footsteps, Reshona."

I felt tears gathering in the corners of my eyes.

"You know, my mother married young. She fell in love very young with a much older man. That was your Grandpa Bo. I didn't think nothin' of it when I was really little, but you know, when I got to be a teen, I did the math. Mama never made like it was a big deal, and of course I wasn't alive when they first got together. But their story, it just kinda seemed regular." Dad cleared his throat and looked at me.

I stared back. Dad had just lost her—my Grandma Ruby—early in 2020. She knew I was pregnant, but she died before I gave birth to my son. Grandpa Bo had just died of COVID. Our family was reeling from both their deaths, which we hadn't been able to completely mourn because of all the health protocols. I didn't know if I was prepared to hear what Dad wanted to say. I studied his heavy shoulders and determined face. He was going to say it, whether or not I was ready.

"Are you hearing me, Reshona?"

"I'm listening, Dad."

He nodded. "Well anyway, I'm not saying what happened with you and Robert was right. He was a married man, of course. And an unfaithful one at that. But in terms of you falling in love with him"—he cleared his throat and nodded at words he hadn't yet said—"I guess that experience, I mean, my mother being so young, it just gave me a certain perspective on your relationship." He sighed.

"Okay…"

"It wasn't okay. It troubled me. But Mama's experience, and the fact that Pa was pastor of our church, it affected my decision-making about your situation. It clouded my judgment. I saw some things in my parents' relationship, stuff my mother went through, you know?"

I didn't know, but I also didn't think Dad was going to be more specific, so I chose not to push him.

"My mother held a lot of her emotions in. And she didn't go anywhere. She stayed there. With us. With her family." Dad pressed his mouth together so hard his lips turned white. "But what happened to you… I wish I could go back in time. I wish I could have changed my thinking. Been just a little braver. Something. Because all this lying, it did bother me. And Robert—" Dad rolled his eyes and shook his head. He balled his fists up in his lap. "It's why I'm ready to take accountability. Whatever that looks like, Reshona. You deserved better. I can't change the past, you know. But I can do better now. And whatever you need to do, you have my blessing, okay?"

"Thanks, Dad." I could see the weight of the entire world on his shoulders. I couldn't tell him that it was okay, because he and I both knew it wasn't okay and *I* wasn't okay. I got up, hugged him, and left the room.

This time of the pandemic and my reliance on my parents during my postpartum period opened us up to discuss things we had lived but never shared. As Mom offered advice about the baby, she confided that she was so nervous and fearful of doing the wrong thing or hurting me when I was born that she often stood aside and watched as Granny changed or bathed me. She spoke words of comfort and encouragement to me, often noting that I had more on my plate than she did when she was a new mother, but she never wanted to directly discuss anything related to how I was preparing for the case against Robert. But apparently, my parents did discuss this between the two of them. During one of our three-way conversations, Dad told me that they had decided he would be the spokesperson for the two of them. He would take the interviews with the federal prosecutors and be the one to take the stand if the case went to trial. Part of what he meant by taking full accountability was standing up for the truth when his inclination was always to stand down. He'd confront his fears and come face-to-face with Robert if he had to.

Dad's spirit was often unsettled, full of everything that our family was facing and the faulty understanding that led him to conclusions he later came to regret. But he also listened to me with an open heart. In every conversation, Dad seemed to shed another layer of secrets and shame, eventually arriving in the safe space of vulnerability.

One day, when I walked past the open door of Mom and Dad's bedroom, I saw Dad sitting at the edge of their bed, his back to me and papers scattered around him. A few minutes later, I passed by again, and Dad was in the same position. I popped my head into the room. "Hey."

Dad turned around. "Hey, yourself." He pulled up one corner of his mouth into a lopsided smile. "Remember this?" He picked up a cap and turned it around. Embroidered with "Salt Lake 2002" and the five Olympic rings, it was signed by Robert and had a personal note to my dad.

"No." I read the note. Robert's words of inspiration always came in clutch. He must have given it to Dad as a souvenir from when he sang the national anthem at the opening of the 2002 Winter Olympics.

"You know the news of what he did to you, with the tape and all, had just come out." Dad sighed. "And then he did *this*." He shook the hat at me.

I nodded. I didn't know about the cap he gave Dad, but I remembered when Robert told me about the Olympics being cool and how honored he was to open it up like that.

"And I don't even know why, Reshona, but I just...I wanted to believe him, you know? That we were his *family*. That he was going to *protect* you. I mean, I didn't trust him! How could I? But I guess I believed that he loved you. I wanted to believe him, anyway." Dad's voice cracked, his face spilling hot, stinging tears. "Why the hell did I believe this man?"

Dad wasn't asking me. He wasn't even asking himself. He was asking God. I sat down and took some deep breaths. *Why* did *he believe him? Because I did? Because of Grandma Ruby and Grandpa Bo?* "Robert is really good at lying," I said, finally. "Really good."

"But I let myself believe that the same man who took *advantage* of you would protect you. Why?" Dad flung the hat to the floor.

I shook my head. I knew why I believed him, but not why Dad did.

He looked at me through glassy eyes. "Because he's R. Kelly, that's why." Dad grabbed his face with his hands as if he were trying to snatch it off.

I wanted to offer Dad some words of comfort, but I didn't have any. Dad's tears felt heavy and awkward for me. I sat there, holding space, for as long as I could. "Dad?"

"Thank you for listening, Reshona."

"Thanks for sharing." Then I stepped out of the room and let him cry.

Eleven months after I did the most amazing and humbling thing in my life, becoming a mother, after recovering from preeclampsia and learning to live with postpartum depression, I did the hardest thing I've ever done. I buried Dad. My *real* daddy. He was a man who was complicated and funny and not always right. But he loved me. And he said sorry for the ways he missed the mark in protecting me from the sharks of this world. Sharks like Robert Kelly.

In the days following his death, I kept wondering why. Our family had suffered so much loss: Mom's mom in 2019, Dad's mom in 2020, and Dad's dad in early 2021. And now, just a few months after Grandpa Bo died, Dad left us unexpectedly. But maybe it wasn't so unexpected. I knew Dad was carrying around his stress and grief like boulders in every pocket. Bogged down as he was, Dad dragged his body from place to place and plopped into his recliner like he was dropping a sack of coal on the ground. His breathing was always labored, and his forehead was always crumpled into a frown, even when he was happy. The only time he looked to be at peace was when he and his grandson took a snooze together, the baby's legs on either side of Dad's belly.

In the days following Dad's sudden passing, as I struggled to get my son down to his nap without his human pacifier, I whispered into his baby face, "*But you need to rest.*" Then God told me that was the reason. Dad needed to rest. From his heartache, his regret, his worry, his stress. God saw Dad's heart and forgave him for his shortcomings. And he called Dad home.

My sworn depositions resumed early in 2021. When Dad died a month and a half before my son was to turn one year old, we had to throw on the emergency brakes. I felt like I was in free fall. Then something happened. The music community showed up for us. And a peace that I couldn't explain came over me. After we celebrated his life and mourned his death for a little while, we felt Dad's spirit urging us to get back on our assignments. He was good. He was at peace. God's grace was sufficient for him and would be sufficient for us, too, on this side of eternity.

I resumed my interviews.

There was one prosecutor who seemed to see my humanity and encouraged me to lean into that when it felt hard to answer. When I had to describe the dehumanizing things that Robert made me do, I'd sometimes look over at her and remind myself, once again, that I wasn't the worst thing that had happened to me. It helped to have a woman in the room. Not that she had had experiences remotely resembling mine. I didn't know anything about her beyond her role as a part of the prosecution's team for this case. But because I knew she saw me, it helped me to stay present. When I looked at her, her returned eye contact reminded me that I was no longer where I was, that talking about what happened to me didn't mean it was happening again. That was why I sent her a picture of me when I was pregnant and another once I had the baby. Because I could tell that she saw I was a whole person and not just a crime victim or whatever slanderous accusations the defense was trying to cook up about me.

Then she was pulled off the case and replaced with another woman. I was shocked and sorry to see her go. In retrospect, I regret my decision to share those two photos of me because it got misconstrued as a friendship and a line that shouldn't have been crossed. Perhaps, in another place and time, we could have been friends. Or maybe not. But I learned a valuable lesson. I had to see my humanity in my *own* eyes and not look for that validation from other people. Yes, the prosecutors were kind. But they were there to do a job. And frankly, so was I.

* * *

Mom had planned not to be directly involved with my family's role in the mounting case against Robert. Now that Dad was deceased, Mom had no choice but to step up and speak to the federal prosecutors for them both. It was around October 2021 when we resumed the meetings with prosecutors, this time with Mom. Everyone knew it was going to be difficult for her. She was a wife in her very earliest stages of grief and a woman who was feisty but also timid about public speaking.

She had been subpoenaed, of course, and she knew that I had been cooperating with the prosecution for the better part of two years and had done over twenty interviews with their team at that point. But Mom's unhealed trauma from the last time we accepted "protection" from the opposing side, combined with her mama-bear tendency to safeguard me from ridicule and our family from retaliation, kept her mentally handcuffed to Robert Sylvester Kelly. At first, she refused to believe that Robert's side was against us. So, in her initial interviews, Mom kept responding that she didn't recall what happened in answer to the prosecution's questions. My lawyer was prepping her like he had prepped me but with little impact. However once I began to sit in on those preparatory sessions, Mom started to face our reality so she could remember the truth. I felt exasperated but also stunned at just how effectively Robert had managed to brainwash her, often through words that came out of my mouth and actions I had been forced to take that crushed her spirit. Without Dad to encourage her, Mom was alone and struggling with all the ways life had changed so quickly and drastically for us.

If our lawyer was part coach and part referee during Mom's actual interviews with the federal prosecutors, then I was Mom's tough-love cheerleader before and after her sessions. We didn't attend each other's interviews, of course. But when our lawyer tried to familiarize her with the types of questions he thought the prosecutors or defense attorneys would ask and Mom became nervous, I tried to give her a context for remembering the truth so she could answer confidently. Thankfully, both Mom and I had been granted immunity for the time we didn't tell the truth to the grand jury in the state's first case against Robert. I knew that was God's mercy. We had to use this opportunity to right that wrong. Mom knew it, too. I realized through this preparation process that Mom had kept her head in the sand about some things when Dad was alive. I guess she saw actual ignorance as safer than knowledge that might require a lie. But it also became clear to us all that Mom did know about quite a few things. It was just that she had previously been coached by Robert and the lawyers he provided us with to give such airtight lies for answers that she had to unlearn those lies so the truth could breathe free.

Life had taught us all the hard lessons of how lies and shame make mountains out of molehills. The things that happened at Robert's command—both to me and to others—were whole mountain ranges. His abuse stole my childhood. But the fear, secrets, and lies surrounding his grooming and abuse of me kept my family in a stranglehold for decades.

If lies could control us, then the truth would free us. Somehow.

CHAPTER 13

JANE DOE SPEAKS

ALL THE PREP AND questioning in the world could not have prepared me to walk into that full courtroom on August 18, 2022. The trial had begun eight days before, and the media called me the federal government's star witness. I was never so happy to have to wear a surgical mask on my face as I was then. I didn't want anyone to see my expression before I pulled myself together: not the spectators who had stood in line for hours for a chance at a seat, or the throngs of reporters clutching their notebooks. Only a few minutes before, I had been sitting in the holding room having what could best be described as a short flu-and–panic attack combination. Though my cousin who had come with me kept reassuring me the room's temperature was warm, my body was shaking violently because I felt like I was in an icebox.

As the bailiff walked me through the courtroom's center aisle, my face felt like a splotchy mess, both too hot and too cold. My mind was jumbled. I wondered if the crowded rows of observers—the groupies, reporters, and #MuteRKelly activists and a few of Robert's current and former supporters—included any folks I knew. Did anyone from high school or my old church see me walk in? Was anyone besides my cousin there to cheer me on? What would my other family members think? I tried to make out the few familiar faces of those who had been interviewing me for so many months in the sea of surgical masks. Not all who had been involved were there, of course. Several prosecutors had changed positions, been taken off the case, or just been swapped out to cover the backlog of federal cases following the worst of the pandemic, so I had gotten a taste of what it was like to have to talk about difficult truths in front of a revolving door of new folks.

The crowd blurred into one big blob as I caught sight of the back of Robert's head. A fresh wave of intimidation washed over me. I had no more loyalty to him, no more love for him. But the idea of facing the man I was never able to confront in front of a courtroom full of people churned up every bad feeling I'd felt because of Robert since I tore myself away from him more than eleven years before:

The pain I tried to minimize, telling myself that we were now friends.

The insecurity behind my fake smile when I hung at the studio or attended his parties.

The trauma of revisiting spaces where I'd been abused and tormented.

The fear that there would always be more videotapes.

The sense of inadequacy when I saw him flanked by other women.

The neediness of wanting to be validated by him.

The shame of being seen as dirty, thirsty, damaged goods.

As I got closer to the witness stand where I was to sit, I walked right past Robert, slumped at the table for the defense. I thought of the years of manipulation, gaslighting, violence, love bombing, isolation, humiliation, and dehumanization, and I sat down. Tried my best not to look at him. But a feeling came over me and convinced me: The most important thing for me to do was to face him, *right now.* I shifted my eyes. Looked. At the moment I did that, he sneered at me, disgust oozing from his expression as if to say I had turned on him.

Disgust? At *me*?

The nerve of you! My mind roared. His arrogant attempt at intimidation limped and died right in front of me. Robert had no power over me. His tired stunt flipped a switch within my spirit so I could access my true source of power and courage. I didn't look at him again.

I took my oath under my chosen pseudonym of Jane Doe. My decision probably didn't make sense to everyone, especially since I had been referred to by my real name in the courtroom proceedings during Robert's first trial in 2008. As I discussed earlier, there were so many ways in which my identity wasn't protected then, but this time, as a single mother and grieving daughter who would testify to Robert's crimes, and with my family name known in Chicago, I didn't want to expose my identity to more folks than necessary and make myself a curiosity. I wasn't ready for the notoriety.

The prosecution took care to ask questions in an unbiased way, and I answered every question I needed to with confidence. But the cross-examination by the lawyers for Derrel McDavid, June Brown, and especially Robert was more grueling. They asked questions that were designed to lead me to the answer they wanted. I answered with the truth. It was difficult to tell a roomful of people about experiences I had previously told myself I would never discuss, but what was also nerve-racking was the fact that I saw Robert get off the first time. So even though I was testifying and exposing everything, I couldn't be sure what the finale would look like. I just kept praying that Robert's time was up.

Even when the answers were embarrassing or made me look needy, I kept my head on straight and stayed faithful to the commitment I made to my dad that I would do the right thing and not be swayed to the left or right. Holding on to the truth, I kept trusting that it would lead to the correct outcome: to revelation and justice.

The US attorney's questions asked to my adult self in the cold light of that full courtroom made it painfully clear that even though I was always following Robert's direction or reacting to what Robert wanted, he *always* had a plan:

Q. Jane, you can take off your mask.

A. Okay. Thank you.

Q. And pull that microphone nice and close. Now, you explained in your testimony earlier today that the conversations changed to sex talk with Mr. Kelly. Do you recall that testimony?

A. Yes.

Q. Can you explain to the jury if you know why you all engaged in sex talk at that time?

A. Again, after he became my godfather, there became an attraction, and he started making advances, and that's how it unfolded.

Q. And why did you engage in the sex talk with him?

A. I just kind of went with the flow. He kind of threw me off. I wasn't exactly sure how to respond or how I should handle it, so I just was being responsive.

Q. And how did you view him, Mr. Kelly, at that time when the sex talk started and you participated in it? How did you view him at that time?

A. As an authoritative figure.

Q. What do you mean? Can you explain that?

A. Well, he was an adult, and he was somebody that I looked up to, so he was an authoritative figure over me at the time, aside from the sexual acts or anything like that. So, again, I went with the flow.

Q. Okay. And then we talked—in your testimony, you explained to the jurors that the—you started to engage in sex acts. And, again, we are talking about before you turned 15 when the sexual intercourse began. Okay. So we're talking about that time frame between—when you were 14 years old.

A. Mm-hmm.

Q. Why—and you said you engaged in sex acts with Mr. Kelly. Why did you participate in those sex acts?

A. It was out of intimidation. And, again, like, he was an authoritative figure, so I didn't know how to respond. I didn't know how to say no. I felt uncomfortable, but at the same token, I looked up to him. I did see him as an authoritative figure, so I just kind of went along with things, and then it somewhat became normal.

Q. Okay. So when you say "it somewhat became normal," what do you mean? What did you start feeling for him?

A. I started having feelings for him. I was attracted to him in that way, and things were happening so frequently, it was kind of just like being done out of repetition.

Q. And when you say things that were happening so frequently, what are you talking about?

A. Sexual involvement, engagement, and our interactions.

Q. Okay. And then—again—so we were talking about the period when you were 14 and sex acts were occurring. And then you explained to the jury that when you were 15, that progressed to sexual intercourse; is that correct?

A. Yes.

Q. And you had explained that you knew you were 15 because you had lost your virginity; is that right?

A. Correct.

Q. And just to be clear, who—to whom did you lose your virginity?

A. Robert.

Q. And how were you feeling about him around that time, when you engaged in—first began engaging in sexual intercourse when you were 15?

A. I developed feelings for him, and I felt good about our interactions.

Q. What are some of the things that, if any, he was saying to make you feel good about your interactions?

A. That he loved me, that he would take care of me, that he was my protector.

Q. And what were your—what were your responses to those—those things that he was saying about being—that he would protect you and that he loved you?

A. I would respond in the same way, "I love you, too," and I would feel good about the level of comfort that he was giving me. So it made me feel good.

Q. And you also talked about—there was a point where you were willing to bring in your friends into the sexual acts and sexual intercourse with Mr. Kelly. Why were you comfortable—I take that back. Why did you do those things?

A. Because I considered myself to be a submissive person and I wanted to give him what he wanted or required.

Q. What were the ways in which you encouraged your friends—again, we were talking about specifically Pinky and Brittany—to join you all in those sex acts?

A. It would start off as like joking conversations of me having a crush on him or just discussing different interactions that me and him had just to gauge like how they might feel or if they would want to be included.

Q. When we were talking about Brittany earlier, you mentioned that she was older than you. How much older than you was Brittany—is Brittany?

A. I believe a year.

Q. So when you engaged—first engaged in sex acts with your—was it your testimony that that occurred when you were 15?

A. Yes.

Q. And so Brittany would have been how old?

A. 16.

Q. And can you please explain to the jury that first experience, if you will, with Brittany, how you engaged her into the sex acts with Mr. Kelly.

A. It would start out with me just joking and saying, like, "Oh, I have a crush on him. He's like—I like his music. I like when he says this with the music or that." It was like things that he would have me to say that would make them—like put something on their minds to be engaged with us.

Q. And can you recall the first instance with Brittany when that—the first time it happened with Brittany?

A. It was at Chicago Trax in the lounge of the studio.

Q. Okay. If you recall, can you just describe that interaction.

A. We were all sitting on the couch after a studio session, watching TV is how we would usually go or maybe listening to some music that had just got finished up, and then we would start by like him saying, "I want to see you do this to Brittany" or "I want to see this or that." And that's when the emotions would start or the interactions would start sexually.

Q. And when you say he was saying, "I want to see you do this" or "I want to see you do that," what were those things? Can you describe them.

A. Kissing, grabbing on each other's breasts or like grinding and holding each other by the waist and like dancing, dance movements.

Q. Okay. And would you do those things as he instructed?

A. Yes.

Q. Why were you willing to do those things?

A. Again, I was thinking I was in love at the time and I was being submissive and I wanted to give him what he wanted and I didn't want to upset him or make him feel like I wasn't cooperating, so I went along with it.

Q. Now, you had mentioned that you had feelings—again, when you were 14 and 15. But you had feelings for him that you loved him; is that right?

A. Yes.

Q. And what, if anything—or some of the things that he was doing at this time when you were 14, 15, and 16 that made it seem like he was—you all were in love with one another?

A. Just the time that he would allow me to be around him, through certain emotions or, like, certain things he would do for me, like, if it was my birthday or if—anything that I wanted, he just made it seem like it was available to me. So not just like materialistic, more like emotional support with anything that I was going through, whether it was school, my group, or friends, he was just there for me. He was supportive.

Q. What about events; did he attend any events that you were participating in?

A. Yes. It would be like if my group was doing something or if I was having like basketball games, things of that nature.

Q. And what would he do at your music groups or basketball games, if anything?

A. He would just show up and be supportive and, you know, it looked really cool from my friends' perspective that I had this celebrity showing up for me. So it was more so like that.

Q. How did that make you feel when he showed up—when he showed up for you?

A. It made me feel good, excited.[3]

I sat on the witness stand clenching the scarf I was wearing so tightly that my palms were sweating. I looked out into the gallery and caught sight of one of Robert's friends. His look of disgust toward me threatened to send my mind into a bad place so I looked away. As I answered still more questions, I realized just how well Robert had groomed me to submit to his will, seek his approval, and make me believe his feelings were more important than mine. He also hid my own best interests from me:

Q. I'd like to direct your attention to April 2000.

Do you recall being interviewed or spoken to by people from the Department of Children and Family Services?

A. Yes.

Q. What do you recall about the encounter?

A. There was an allegation made about the nature of Robert and I—excuse me—the nature of Robert and I's relationship, and they wanted to come out and ask questions to investigate if there was anything sexual happening between us.

Q. And in 2000—April 2000 you were still 15; is that right? You turned 16 in April of—I'm sorry—in September of 2000; is that right?

A. Yes.

Q. Okay. So April 2000 you were 15 years old. What was your response to the questioning from DC—from the Department of Children and Family Services about their allegations?

A. I denied it.

Q. Why did you deny it?

A. I was afraid that something bad would happen to Robert. He really instilled that in me, if anybody found out about the nature of our relationship, that things would be really bad for him, and I wanted to protect him, so I did everything I could to keep that a secret.

Q. So you were—just to be clear, you were untruthful with the Department of Children and Family Services; is that right?

A. Yes.

Q. And you testified that you wanted to protect him?

A. Yes.

Q. Why did you want to protect him?

A. Well, again, I did look up to him. I didn't want to see anything bad happen to him, and at this point with the way things were happening between us, I was also afraid.

Q. Afraid of what?

A. I didn't want to upset him, I didn't want to trigger anything, and I didn't want to expose what was happening between us.

Q. Did you want to keep your relationship intact?

A. I did.

Q. Now, at this time—again, this is April of 2000, you

were 15 years old—did you tell your parents about what was happening between you and Robert Kelly?

A. No.

Q. Why?

A. Because that was something that I would take to my grave. I was not going to reveal that to anybody after many conversations of him drilling how important it was that he would be in big trouble if anybody found out about this, so I looked at it as I was protecting him.

Q. Did you feel comfortable telling your parents that you were engaging in sexual activity with Robert Kelly at that time? Again, this is April 2000.

A. No.

Q. Why?

A. Because I knew it was something they wouldn't approve of.

Q. Now, after that, you were approached and questioned by Department of Children and Family Services. You were later questioned by Chicago Police Department officers; is that correct?

A. Yes.

Q. And what—what were they asking you about? What were they questioning you about?

A. Robert and I's relationship, have we had any sexual contact with each other.

Q. What was your response to that questioning?

A. No.

Q. Why did you respond that way?

A. Because, again, I just—it was embedded in me that this could never come out, and I didn't want my parents to find out, either, so I was doing everything I could to keep it a secret.

Q. Did you tell Mr. Kelly about CPD questioning you?

A. Yes.

Q. What was his response?

A. He was just asking what type of questions they were asking, asking me how did I answer the questions, and he was telling me that I did a good job and that I handled everything correctly.[4]

As challenging as it was to answer the prosecution's questions, sitting for cross-examination by Robert's lawyer was even more uncomfortable. It was the second day of my testimony, and I felt exposed. I was trying to focus on one question at a time, not over-explaining and not underexplaining, but just trying to address exactly what she asked me.

When she began to show me transcripts of texts Robert and I had exchanged in 2018 and 2019, I felt especially intimidated. I winced as I answered yes, I sent and recognized them. Not only was I afraid of how I looked to the jury and spectators, but I was ashamed to answer some of the questions, whether it was on behalf of me or my parents.

> **Q.** Now, after you moved out, you maintained a very tight relationship with Robert, didn't you?
>
> **A.** Yes.
>
> **Q.** Despite how terribly abusive it was, according to you, you remained close to him, correct?
>
> **A.** He wasn't like that all the time.
>
> **Q.** Uh-huh. In fact, your whole family was very close to him—
>
> **A.** Yes.
>
> **Q.** —even—even after you broke up because of this alleged abusive relationship, right?
>
> **A.** Yes.[5]

Sometimes I answered meekly, embarrassed by her question and ashamed to hear myself answer out loud. On the face of her question, I knew she wanted to make the jury doubt me, to show that Robert must not have been so bad if I still reached out to him and cared about him.

Q. On October 15, 2018, you said, "My mom lost her mother. Check on her when you get a moment, please." Right?

A. Yes.

Q. Because Mr. Kelly was close to your mother, right?

A. Yes.

Q. Even at this point; isn't that fair? That's correct, right?

A. Yes.

Q. And he responded a little bit later, and he said, "Wow, I just got this. Sorry to hear that. Send me her number, please," which you did, right?

A. Yes.

Q. And he said, "I'm okay. How are you doing?" And you said, "My heart is heavy, but it will get better with time," right?

A. Correct.

Q. Then you asked him, "What have you been up to?" And he gave you—he said, "I understand you're talking to the mirror right now, but you're right, it will all get better if you really believe that like I do." And you responded, "I can only imagine. I think about you and pray for you often." He responded, "And it's working. I appreciate it." And you said, "I feel—I feel it, so I know you do." And then you said, "Let me know when you can catch up." Go to the next page. And you said, "Okay"—and he said, "Okay, baby. Just stay on my radar. It's all good." And you said, "Will do."[6]

It was difficult to have to admit that yes, I did go along with this or say that. But on a deeper level, I wasn't just facing the courtroom or Robert. I was facing myself as well.

Q. And then you hit him up again on January 3. "What you doing tonight?" Do you see the top one?

A. Yes.

Q. And he says, "Studio session, but I will be there drinking and chilling." And you said, "Okay. I'm going to come through." "Come through" means "I'm going to stop by," right?

A. Correct.

Q. And he said, "Hit me around 8:30 or 9:00."

And then you texted him later and said, "Are you there?" You said, "Need you to respond right away." Right?

A. Correct.

Q. "Hey, are you there? We're pulling up now." And then he didn't respond, right?

A. Correct.

Q. And then later on, he said, "What happened?" And you said, "I came. You never responded, and I kept calling your phone while I was outside." Do you remember that night?

A. Not exactly, but that sounds about right.

Q. And then he said, "Oh, my God, are you serious? Why not do what everybody else does. Just come in. LOL. It's a party. I can't hear my phone. People grabbing on me trying to take pictures."[7]

I wanted to believe that the man who could be this thoughtful and fun person had canceled out the man who had stolen my virginity, my agency, and my self-esteem. I wanted to believe that if that terrible version of Robert ever existed, he no longer did because I had somehow brought out the best in him.

I still wanted to believe that I was important to him. Necessary, even. That I had the ability to do something for him that no one else could. Without me even realizing it, after I took a pause and caught my breath, I had created a new job for myself: reminding Robert why he loved me so he would be kind to me, and rehabbing his image in my own mind.

I doubt that it was Robert's lawyer's intent, but so much of what she forced me to confront in her cross-examination was like a crash course in my own state of mind just three short years before. I had a kind of revelation. By 2019, I thought I had washed Robert out of my hair more than I actually had. Having my text messages thrown back in my face was like a window into my broken heart. I wanted to be healed. I wanted to believe that I was all right, that what had happened wasn't as bad as it was. I know now that I was just coping, trying to make lemonade from the sack of lemons Robert had thrown into my arms when I was a girl.

As I sat on the witness stand, I had a flash of clarity about the intentional work I needed to do in order to repair the damage that had been done by Robert and discover the woman I was and wanted to be. I was a mother now. I wanted my son to love himself for who God made him to be, not because of who someone else said he was. But I needed to be able to model that. On the other side of this experience, I determined that I would get there.

While this realization couldn't be captured in my answers to every question in the courtroom, I knew that what I said registered. I knew I was no longer the nasty girl or the girl on the videotape that got peed on. It was bigger than me at that point.

When I finally finished with my two grueling days of testimony, I made sure I looked at Robert before I walked out of the courtroom. I felt as light as a feather, like I could wash my hands of him. When I walked back into that holding room, I literally fell to the ground and cried. I lay there for a moment as the prosecutors congratulated me: *You did great! You did not fold!* I *knew* everything would be okay. I didn't feel scared anymore. I didn't feel attacked anymore. It felt spiritual, like oil was running off my body.

I thought about how day two of my testimony had begun: the bailiff escorting me to the witness stand, me feeling so nervous and discombobulated, while folks passing by mistook me for the lawyer. They didn't see me as a victim. That was when Dad's spirit had come over me and stayed by my side. I heard the things he used to say to speak life into me. I felt his protection. There, on the other side of eternity, he reached out to me and redeemed himself by giving me the courage and the authority to speak the way I needed to. And I did.

Following my testimony, I felt some trepidation even though I had given it as Jane Doe. Chicago is a very small city with a long memory, and I'm known here. I didn't know how I'd be received following this new exposure. Would I be safe walking into a restaurant or going to work? Would my coworkers who liked to blast music to greet all who entered the building still keep Robert's songs in heavy rotation? Would I still be triggered if they did? Would the internet trolls still tag me in photos or videos and attach crude threats? But even with these concerns, I felt a new kind of courage within me. I had faced Goliath and no longer had anything to hide. Mom had done the same. Going into her testimony, she had been very prayerful and was relieved that she had stayed calm, spoken the truth for her and my dad, and no longer felt like she had to live a lie because of fear-driven loyalty. She said it felt like she had regained space in her brain once she released Robert's big lie.

The verdict came down: guilty on numerous counts of producing child sexual abuse videos and coercing minors into criminal sexual activity. It was confirmation of what I already knew, a burden lifted. It was no surprise that folks had their opinions: about me, the trial, the verdict. But their opinions of me didn't matter because I knew

I wouldn't have to deal with Robert's lies anymore. I wouldn't have to rebuild my life from rock bottom again. I finally felt free to be myself. I was no longer hiding. I could move on, enjoy time with my son, and pursue whatever career path I wanted without this lingering over my head.

On the day of Robert's sentencing, February 23, 2023, I gave myself permission to not attend. I was relieved that Robert had been found guilty in both his federal cases, and hopeful that justice would be served through a long prison sentence. It had been excruciating to write my victim impact statement, but I knew it was necessary for my own sense of closure. However, once I had written it, I didn't feel the need to be present to read it. Instead, I chose to allow my lawyer to do that so that I could preserve my peace. Robert was someone from my past who would never be a part of my future, so I decided not to give him one more chance to sneer at me and try to get into my head.

> As I reflect on the thought of preparing this statement, my hands begin to shake and my heart pounds in my chest. Just writing this is stressful. When I think of all that I have lost due to Robert Kelly, all I can do is cry. I have lost my dignity due to Robert Kelly. I have lost my dreams due to Robert Kelly. I have lost my teenage years due to Robert Kelly. I have lost my father due to Robert Kelly. And I almost lost my entire family due to suicidal thoughts caused by Robert Kelly. I will never get back what Robert Kelly took from me.

As a teenager, I wanted to be a star. Music was my life. And I loved performing. I really believed I had a future as a recording artist. I never thought that my first love, music, would lead to the darkness that I experienced for over a decade and almost killed me.

When your virginity is taken by a pedophile at the age of 14 and you live for him, your life is never your own. I don't know how Robert Kelly was able to obtain so much power over me. At first I believed he could help me in my music career, and that he cared about me. That could not have been more wrong.

During my teenage years, I had sex with Robert Kelly hundreds of times, even when I didn't want to. It is still disturbing to me that millions of people have seen the sex tape that Robert made of me as a child. I will never be able to unsee, unthink, or be unaffected by the child pornography in which I was enticed to engage in.

I thought Robert loved me. To do the things he did, he, in fact, loathed me. I can't imagine treating anyone that I love the way that Robert treated me. Looking back at it, I was only one of the girls, women to be abused by Robert. I didn't realize until I graduated from high school that I didn't make music for years while Robert was in my life. And that was the main reason I began to associate with Robert.

Robert was abusive and dominating. The rules that I was forced to follow for years because I believed I needed Robert were degrading. Sometimes I couldn't eat for days. Sometimes I couldn't go to the bathroom without his permission. Sometimes I had to go to the bathroom in a bucket. Sometimes I had to have sex with women. It's hard to believe that Robert had that much power over me. Robert knowingly victimized me as a child. I was brainwashed by Robert and a sex slave. He had no remorse, and history has shown that there were women after me who suffered the same fate.

Robert made me suicidal as a young adult. It is awful being me. I gave up my family for him. Nothing else mattered back then. And I still don't know why. I love music. But by the time I was 16, 17 years of age, the only thing that mattered was him. I was manipulated, and independence didn't seem like an option. Robert shattered me.

I need closure. And I need Robert Kelly in jail for as long as the law will allow. He shouldn't be able to harm anyone ever again. I wish I was strong enough to speak up sooner. I just didn't have the strength. I have been permanently scarred by Robert emotionally, physically, mentally, and socially. I will forever be the girl that R. Kelly pissed on. Every time I walk into a room, it feels like the child pornography tapes arrive a couple minutes before I do. I am rarely seen. Child pornography tapes have predetermined the attraction that I have with society. I keep a small circle because Robert has proved to me that I can't trust many people.

I am 38 years old and learned sex through the lens of a pedophile. I have never had a loving romantic relationship with a man that lasted longer than a year. I have been bullied on social media and looked upon as the problem because I was victimized as the child. In what world does that make sense? Despite all of the things that Robert did to me, today members of his team and those that support him still attack me.

There are documented tapes establishing the horrible experiences that are actually my life. The public sees child pornography. The world does not see the depression and the thoughts in my mind that would give anyone pause that I could ever lead a normal life. I have never been able to experience normal. My teenage years and adulthood have been built through the lens of a pedophile. It is awful living life not knowing that you can't trust yourself because you are unaware exactly how fractured and broken you are. No amount of therapy will make me normal. The best I can hope for is to properly function and deal with the brokenness that is my life. Is that fair? But if you ask Robert Kelly's team, I am the problem, I am deceitful, I am the liar.

Let me be clear. Robert Kelly is no saint. Does anyone really believe that Robert is not in those child pornography tapes? Does anyone believe Robert did not entice a young girl and destroy her life? Does anyone believe what happened to me was okay? I think the answer is no. But if I was to listen to Robert's team, I would be the 14-year-old girl, again, being enticed to continue down a socially destructive path and the pedophile will still be in control of my life.

> I made the decision some years ago to take control of my broken life. It is extremely hard, but it's the only life I have. I make decisions in my own time frame. I try to review all the possible results with as much certainty as possible before I decide what to do. It only seems right. I try to be more methodical because following passion for my first love, music, broke me beyond repair. Another mistake like that will kill me. Robert is not worth dying over.
>
> I cannot escape the psychological prison Robert has put me in. Robert Kelly needs to be in jail for the balance of his natural born life.[8]

As I read my victim impact statement for the writing of this book, I felt sad that I believed I was broken beyond repair. Yes, Robert did break me. He cracked my body open and scrambled my understanding of who I was. But I gave him too much credit, because he did not and will *never* have the last word on me. He can't break my soul.

CHAPTER 14

THE BLOOD

GROWING UP AS AN Edwards *and* a Landfair was a full-time job, one I was happy to have. On Sundays, I didn't just share the church pew with my cousins as Grandpa Bo preached the word and Bo/P (mom's dad) kept a watchful eye on us as a deacon. After Sunday service, we'd all go to Sunday dinner at Grandma Ruby's. Any weekday could find me at the dining room table with extended family or getting my hair braided by a cousin. On the weekends, Bo/P and Granny's den was the place to be for rambunctious conversation, laughter, and good food. In the summers, there was the annual Fourth of July family cookout hosted by the Edwards and Landfair families on alternate years, as well as road trips to Mississippi for family reunions.

Both the Edwards and Landfair sides of my family run deep in Chicago, our ancestors having arrived with the waves of Black migration from Jackson and Lexington, Mississippi, in the 1950s. When my mom was coming up, folks would joke that when you saw one Edwards sister, you saw three. They were that close. Decades before I ever sang with my cousins in 4 The Cause, the Edwards Singers—a gospel group composed of Mom, Sparkle, and their brothers and sisters—sang at every family program and many Chicagoland churches. And the Landfairs. If you thought you could pick a fight with my dad because he was short, you had better be ready to fight *all* the Landfair boys, the brothers as well as the cousins. They didn't play that.

Mom and Dad grew up with each other at church; that was how they met and fell in love when they were teens. They were each other's one true love, and their high school romance surprised no one. Before they were twenty years old, my parents were married and had me. Two strong families had come together to create a family that they believed no man could ever pull apart. While my parents remained rock-solid in their marriage until my dad passed away, one man did pull our family asunder, leaving broken pieces of what we had been in shards on the ground. Shards that cut and could draw blood. Robert Sylvester Kelly shattered my family—which had been my place of identity, safety, and possibility—by first infiltrating it. This is why I know Robert is the villain in the story of my life.

I thought that when I became his goddaughter, I had become a part of *his* family, and my family was happy to embrace his, whether in the body of Christ or as down-to-earth folks right here in Chicago. But we *never* became family to Robert. We were just gullible enough to believe he had become family to *us*.

But how?

With my family, Robert smelled blood. And like any good predator, he didn't pounce immediately. Sparkle was his first point of contact; in her, he saw a talented singer hungry for her own crack at fame. When he met her family—folks who were working musicians even further away from the limelight than she was—Robert knew he had hit the jackpot. And I was his perfect prey: an ambitious and starstruck twelve-year-old girl who loved Jesus and knew how to obey adults.

My family was full of all the imperfections you can find in many families, but we were blind to our own weaknesses. We thought we were strong enough and loyal enough to withstand the power of a slick but beloved superstar. No shade to second chances and finding Jesus, but I doubt that Robert's marriage to Andrea and his publicly giving his life to Christ had convinced everyone that Robert was a 100 percent–changed man.

We thought that Robert was the answer to our collective prayer. (In all honesty, I *never* asked God if he had sent Robert our way. I don't know *what* my other family members did.) Instead, he was the opposite. He poisoned the blood we shared, straining the relationship between Mom and Sparkle as well as Sparkle and me. He grew in significance within our family unit like a tumor that grows undetected at first, until it gets so large that it's all we can think about. Of course, the power and celebrity of the R. Kelly brand was so big that it was hard to break ranks with, especially since we were musicians in Chicago who didn't want to be frozen out of the local music scene. This was one point of contention when things broke bad with him and Sparkle.

And about that, I've come to realize three things about the situation that supposedly caused the rift between Sparkle and Robert that were lost on me when I was thirteen:

1. I should never have been entrusted with an "adult" secret that had such high stakes.
2. Robert already knew the answer to his question. His bit of theater was designed to poison Sparkle's mind and make me feel guilty that her misfortune was "my fault."

3. He used the incident as a loyalty test to see if I could keep secrets.

Yes, Robert had been abused as a child. He told me all about how much those terrible experiences hurt and confused him as he lay his head upon my naked girl's breasts. I don't doubt that his abuse stunted his own emotional growth, gave him an unhealthy relationship to sex and love, and made him prone to abuse others. But Robert the adult didn't seek help. With the hundreds of millions of dollars that flowed through his Chocolate Factory, he never chose to raise awareness of child sexual abuse or at least get any meaningful help for himself. From the folks on his personal payroll to the executives at Jive Records, everyone was turning a blind eye to Robert's addiction and hitching themselves to his rising star. When the Aaliyah marriage story broke, Robert could have hired the *best* PR people in the world to create a campaign to raise awareness about child sexual abuse, mental health, anything. And folks would have loved him even more for his transparency. Sure, it would have been a risky move, but secretly marrying a fifteen-year-old rising star under false pretenses was risky. So what the hell!

Some of you want to give Robert a pass. He was a hurting man. My parents should have done better. And, to your mind, I was clearly a pathological liar who wanted to have my cake and eat it too. But if a rich and powerful grown-ass man can be hurting (Robert was twenty-nine when he met twelve-year-old me), then couldn't *I* be hurting? If you can have sympathy for the things that went wrong in his upbringing, then can't you say that maybe I was vulnerable myself, due in part to some of my inputs and experiences?

None of the missed cues and the poor decisions made by the adults around me excuses Robert Kelly from grooming me sexually, manipulating me, and abusing me emotionally and physically. *He* did that. Sparkle didn't and my parents didn't. What they did was trust him for no good reason, allowing him a level of access to me that would have been unthinkable if he were just a regular Joe who made beats.

Robert became a puppeteer, and the members of my immediate and even extended family became his puppets.

When I was going on sixteen, I was in my family's Ford Explorer truck with my parents. Robert had been out of town for several weeks—I think he had been on tour—and now that he was back, my parents were dropping me off at his house for a sleepover with the kids. This was around 2000, and our truck had one of those old brick-like car phones, the kind built into the center console between the driver and passenger seats that could be used only as a speakerphone. Anyway, the phone rang, and it was Robert. My stomach filled with butterflies at the sound of his voice.

"Hey, Rob," Dad answered, his eyes trained on the road.

"Wassup, G," Robert responded. It was clear that Robert hadn't asked a question, so Dad didn't give an answer. He talked shop about something or other, probably about some session work Robert wanted to do quickly to capture the inspiration he had while on the road. I wasn't really paying attention to what they discussed. My dad had the same deferential tone he always had with Robert, but something about Robert's confidence and unrehearsed authority took up space even though he wasn't in the car with us. I wanted to hug the feeling of his presence.

"So you headed over now with Sho?"

"Yes. She's in the car now." Dad nodded at the late-day sun streaming through the windshield.

"You been listenin' to grown-man talk, Sho?"

I chuckled. "The phone is a speakerphone!" My tone playful, I stopped short before saying "Daddy" like I would have if we were alone.

"True dat." Robert smiled through the phone. I wondered if Mom and Dad could hear that. "Can't wait to tell you about being on tour. I know you wanna do that yourself. I mean, you done it in Europe and all, but American crowds are different for sure."

"I can't wait." I tried not to sound too breathless.

We chatted a bit more, but I was so full of wanting to see him that I couldn't think of much else.

"All right, Sho. We all gonna see you soon, then. The kids been asking about you."

"Okay." I sighed. "I love you! I miss you!" My voice was singsong-y, and I stretched out the *you* in the silly way I sometimes talked to him when we were feeling flirty.

"Yup, me too, Sho! Like I said, the kids been missing their best playmate, you know."

We got off the phone and it was only then that I noticed how thick the air was in the truck. My parents had been dead silent as I talked to Robert.

"You talkin' to him like that's your man!" Mom's tone had an accusatory edge, one she usually reserved for when she talked quietly and then laughed loudly with her sisters in their parents' den.

Seeing Dad's eyes glance at me through the rearview mirror made me cast mine down. I chomped down on the nub of a nail still left on my middle finger. It started to bleed. I clamped my mouth around it quickly, my saliva mixing with blood as I tried to soothe the pain. I had slipped up and I knew it. I had been so caught up in missing Robert and the excitement that coursed through me at hearing his voice that I had forgotten my captive audience in the truck with me. So from that moment forward, I felt like it was kind of obvious what was up between Robert and me, though of course I didn't discuss anything with my parents until I was forced to a year later. But in subsequent drop-offs to Robert's house, my dad would often seem uncomfortable, like he was doing it under duress.

I could see in Dad's eyes that he wanted to speak up or say *something*, but he was a passive, nonconfrontational person, almost to a fault. Remember how I said the Landfair boys would kick folks' butts if they messed with Dad? Well, Dad wasn't like his brothers and cousins. And without them, he never seemed to be able to stand up to bullies. And Robert was a bully to Dad in addition to being his boss and an authority figure who had power over him. Dad was only three years older than Robert, but their physiques couldn't have been more different. Dad was very short and hefty while Robert looked like he'd just come from lifting or playing a game of pickup basketball. At the studio, Robert and others would poke fun at my dad's size. Dad would laugh it off to save face in front of the folks there, but whenever I witnessed this kind of thing, I could read the discomfort in Dad's energy.

I'll be painfully honest and say that Dad was intimidated by Robert. No, Dad never used those words. At least not with me. But even then, when I was a teen, I could tell that my dad didn't feel empowered to act on what he had to know and what was clearly troubling him about my connection to Robert. Even then, when I was in the thick of it and not wanting things to end with Robert, there was a part of me that wished my dad could fight for me. As it was, Robert was the one who continually filled my ears with how he was fighting for our love, and that he was the only one who could protect me. As I reflect on all that, I recognize that Robert knew my dad was intimidated too, so he used that to constantly draw a comparison between himself and my dad, without even saying a word. It was like he was emasculating him. Robert made me call him "Daddy," claimed the role as my disciplinarian and protector as much as he did my lover. He shaped my view of the world, told me how to interact with every member of my family and non family, and remolded my understanding of myself to become Robert's subservient lover supposedly chosen by God himself. Even though Robert seemed to have a decent relationship with my dad and acted like he liked him more than he did my mom, in reality, he wanted to make my dad irrelevant. Of course, I still loved my dad. I love him now.

I'm writing through tears because Dad was always my North Star, even in my darkest hours. He was a man of strong faith and deep love. He was an artist. And he loved me without conditions. But Robert succeeded in dimming Dad's light, and at the time, I couldn't see it for what it was. All I could see was that Robert would fight to have me even if it hurt me, and Dad couldn't fight back.

In the middle of writing this book, I learned something from one of my cousins who used to be really close to my dad. He told me that one day shortly before Robert's first trial in 2008 was to begin, my dad came over and had a conversation with the Landfair men: his brothers, cousins, and uncles. He asked them for their help in protecting Robert, because, in his heart, he believed he was protecting *me*. Before Dad made that big ask, he balled up his fists really tight, dropped his head, and started pounding his chest hard as he repeated, "I know it's my fault. I know it's my fault." Dad knew there was strength in his brotherhood of Landfair men, but still he feared Robert more. But just imagine if they had put their heads together and made Dad's righteous cause—saving me from Robert—their own?

Writing this book has given me an opportunity to bring my full-grown understanding to a situation I lived as a teenager and new adult. I'm more clear-eyed. I know more about life than I did then. I'm older now than my parents were when they were dealing with my miserable situation. With the wisdom I now have, I realize that my parents were unable to save me because they didn't know they could be saviors. Their ability to see beyond my tantrums, threats, and demands was blocked. I believe they also feared for themselves. They feared being exposed for the ways they had missed the signs, turned a blind eye, and asked God to bless our mess rather than order our steps.

Many R. Kelly fans like to say my family was paid off by Robert. That he bought our silence with money and trips and whatever else. I can see how it could look that way from the outside looking in, but that explanation is too simplistic. But I'll say this about myself: When I was in deep with Robert, I believed that I was his lover and that he gave me things as a sign of his affection for me. Lots of people in abusive relationships think as I did. But his gifts weren't tokens of love; they were tools of manipulation. I also felt that I deserved those nice things because I had experienced so much hell at his hands. In my mind, it was like he owed me that. But now I see that it was another form of manipulation to keep me confused, invested, and stroking his fragile ego. I can't psychoanalyze him, but what I know is that Robert Kelly wasn't and still isn't a healthy and confident man, even though his music catalog would make you think otherwise.

R. Kelly the persona was a caricature of the self-assured man he wanted his fans to believe he was. R. Kelly would thrust his pelvis at the crowd of adoring fans, sing about his sex life, and writhe on the stage with women who couldn't get enough of him. But Robert Kelly the man was insecure and broken, and he would use the money, power, and fame of R. Kelly to bury his own pain and keep vulnerable women and girls, as well as the men on his payroll, in line. The men did his bidding, and the girls, young women, and even a few boys were served to him on a platter.

Some of you remember the babies you made to his music and cried when your kids sang "I Believe I Can Fly" at their fifth-grade graduations. So many of you loved R. Kelly and still do because his music was the soundtrack to your life. Robert's genius—the musical genius that Sparkle kept talking about—was his ability to write a song that was so catchy and relatable that it was worse than an earworm; it was like giving an addict another hit of their poison of choice. That's why some of you still can't let go of his music. It just means too much to you.

We can all like the music we want to like. I can't make anyone put down their R. Kelly crack pipe. But just know that you're not the only one with memories of those songs. I have memories of them too. He wrote several of them while he was being sexually intimate with *me*. When I was a *child*. Robert would pause, sometimes to adjust the video camera that taped our sexual encounters and sometimes to sing a piece of a new song idea into his recorder. I was his source of inspiration, he said. My body was used and exploited by him to birth hit songs that became like crack to the R&B-loving community for decades.

* * *

Mom is still here. She has had a front-row seat to the portion of my life Dad didn't get to witness in the flesh. We've been leaning on each other more. It's also been challenging to navigate this road as mother and daughter, grandmother and mother. Beyond being my mother's daughter, I am a woman. I've had different inputs and experiences than she has, and of course some of those are experiences for which she feels responsibility and harbors regret. It has sometimes felt like Mom has been trying for a do-over. When I get in my feelings, I don't want to hear it. I'm no longer twelve.

It was one of those hard days. Several coworkers had been stepping in the name of love in the breakroom, and I came home to my mother—sitting on the floor beside my toddler son—chewing bubblegum and trying to get him to blow a bubble like hers.

"He doesn't need to be doing that," I said to her in greeting.

"Of course he does. You *like* doing what Granny does, don't you?" She blew an even bigger bubble, to his delight.

"He's *three*." I shook my head.

"I know my grandbaby's age." She blew another bubble.

Mimicking her, he blew a tiny bubble before the effort of blowing landed the entire wad of gum on the floor. He grabbed it quickly and shoved it back in his mouth.

Walking over to them, I frowned at the sprinkles of spittle and damp smudges all over him and everything near him. It was clearly not the first time that same wad of bubblegum went flying. "Did you two at least eat the steamed broccoli I've been trying to get him to eat all week? *Before* chewing bubblegum?"

Mom turned around and looked at me. "Is something wrong, Reshona?" She waited for my response.

I didn't feel like talking about the afternoon dance session that I refused to join. "Today sucked, that's all."

She turned back around and blew a tiny bubble close to his face. She made her face radiate light. He reached out his sticky hands to grab her bubble, so she gulped it back into her mouth. "Best not to bring that attitude into the house, Reshona. We've been having a *great* day."

"But I haven't been, okay? Does my son only get to know about his grandmother's feelings and not his mother's?"

"That's not what I'm saying, Reshona."

I walked over to my son and picked him up with a hug. "I guess I'm confused about what you're saying." Mom had become the poster child for being an overbearing and overprotective grandmother, and it all felt like too much. But I needed her babysitting support and willingness to drop everything for her grandson. I *appreciated* it. Truly. It's just that I also needed to be my child's mother, not just my mother's daughter.

I sat him back down and packed a couple of books, a juice box, and some cheese crackers into a bag. "I think he needs a playdate." I said it like this was as evident to Mom as it was to me.

It wasn't. She scrunched up her face. "He's been playing all day."

"And we need our own date. You and me." I nodded matter-of-factly.

We dropped him off with a relative and found a coffee shop nearby.

I was in the early stages of writing this book and my emotions were raw. I knew I'd be opening up old wounds, but I wasn't prepared for how quickly my coworkers' addiction to Robert's music could trigger emotional whiplash. And my mom's brand of hypervigilant grandparenting triggered it too. I said as much.

"Reshona, I'm just trying to be the best granny I can be. G-Pop too, since Greg is no longer here."

I shook my head. "You *can't* be G-Pop. There's no being Dad, Mom. But when you undermine me as my own son's mother, it just makes him not respect me."

"That's not what I mean to do."

"Well, then stop. Because that's what you're doing." I rolled my eyes. The way she treated me made me regress into my teenage brain, the one that lacked the good sense of the grown woman I was. I paused, breathed, and—feeling my dad's spirit tap me on the shoulder—prayed for patience. "Look, Mom, I know you love him. I know you want everything to be perfect. You, me, life in general. But there *is* no perfect. And we're not doing him any favors by making him think that anything less than wall-to-wall fun, treats, and perfect days is a total disaster. I don't want to teach him something about life that's not true." I felt satisfied that I had made my point respectfully but clearly.

Mom nodded. "I'm not trying to be perfect. I'm just trying to be better." Her voice cracking on the last syllable, Mom picked up her cup and sipped her tea, her other hand resting on the table near mine. Our hands found each other. I saw the glassiness in her eyes and knew that mine had to look the same.

"Sometimes, when I think back to when you were little, Reshona, it's like..." She shook her head. "I just wonder if I had any sense at all. Common sense, I mean. I feel bad. Because I failed you. Greg felt it, too. But as your mother, as a *woman*, I just was supposed to know some things. And I didn't seem to know them." She squeezed her eyes shut, pushing tears out each corner. "And now you're writing this book. And you *should*. You should do whatever you need to do to heal. I'm not standing in the way of that at all."

"You're right, Mom. That's why I'm writing it. Because I want to claim my own voice and my own healing. And I don't need anybody to say it's okay to do. This is *my* life, Mom. I only get this one! So I get to say what it is, what I've learned. I get to tell people who Reshona Landfair is instead of everybody else telling *me*."

"I hear that, Reshona. As a *woman*, I hear that. Write your book. Scream from the top of the Sears Tower. Do whatever you need to do. What I'm saying to you isn't about the *book*, Reshona. But I just don't know how to show you how sorry I am. It's about *me* not being able to make up all those years for *you*. When you deserved better than you got. But if I can love on your little boy, maybe you'll know I'm sorry. And with Greg gone, too, I'm trying to say sorry for the two of us. To *show* you."

She dabbed at her eyes while I let my tears flow.

Mom never planned to be a young widow.

You are here. Mom. Grandmother. Sister. Daughter. Child of God. You continue to evolve in how you define each. I'm learning from you. You were never called to be perfect. Just faithful. But fear crept in and overshadowed your faith. Through you, I know what it feels like to grow. What forgiveness looks like. What acceptance means. How to lay your burdens down. That mothering is an exercise in humility. You are looking for a path forward. Looking for a way to walk into the sun without fear. May you find it, Mom. The path is there, but you must start walking to make it. Faith will guide you. It will make the hard places bearable. You're stronger than you think you are.

Mom has loved me imperfectly and with all she has.

* * *

While the passage of time has softened the sharp edges of our hard feelings, our family hasn't truly healed. It hurts my heart that my abuse was like a wrecking ball in my family, making all the people I love feel like they had to choose sides. I know Mom laments some of what she and my dad did and didn't do. I also believe Sparkle has regrets about what ultimately happened to me.

But life moves forward, not backward.

I am grateful that I have come so far in my own healing, but I realize that it's a lifelong journey. Perhaps my words—the wisdom, knowledge, and understanding that I now have—will help others to seek healing, ask for forgiveness, and access God-given courage to have hard conversations. I love you. I love me, too.

CHAPTER 15

GRACE NOTE

Dear Beautiful Soul,

It's you. It's always been you.

You were the girl with saucers for eyes, and the world was a buffet spread out in front of you. You were the girl who spit rhymes and played basketball with all you had. You loved your parents and especially your baby brother. You loved going to church. You were a friend.

Reshona Landfair. Don't believe yourself not to be good enough. There is no yardstick for good enough. You were a girl, a perfectly imperfect human being. You could not have lived your life in reverse. There was no way for you to know what you know now. So, if you don't remember anything else, remember that children don't protect themselves from danger.

How could you have known there were sharks in the water where you swam? No one posted signs. When he nibbled at your toes, you didn't know he wanted to suck the marrow from your bones. It felt exciting at first. Adultish. You didn't understand how something so wrong could feel so right. You were a girl being saddled with the wants and whims of an adult. A predator who made your injury your own fault. It wasn't.

You were not responsible for breaking up the family. You did not disrupt someone else's life or career. Your narrow shoulders could never bear the blame for what happened, no matter how many voices may have tried to convince you otherwise.

You survived the years of being teased, mocked, and feeling like an outcast. You are healing. Don't be ashamed of your scars. You can cover them if you want to, but you don't have to hide them. You are not the worst thing that happened to you. You are so much more: fearfully and wonderfully made. Beauty for ashes is your new reality.

You are a grown woman now. A woman older than your mother and aunt when you were a teenager. And now that you are here, you realize that you never allowed yourself to imagine your life after forty. It felt too scary because so much of your life was his life and you were afraid you would never have your happily ever after with him. So you just wouldn't let yourself think that far. God knows, just keeping up with the secrets and lies that then made up your life filled every square inch of space in your brain and claimed all the oxygen in every room. How could you think decades into the future?

Well, you're here now. You're good now. Your life isn't perfect, but you've learned that there is no perfect life. And that's okay. Your life is yours. Your thoughts, your dreams, your successes and failures are all yours. You have a son who is the light of your life. You've known love as an adult, but you're still learning what you want in a healthy and long-term relationship. Some days, you want that for yourself, but you know that a relationship with a man can't define and won't complete you. Your biggest pursuit: Being the woman you were created to be. Being whole and healthy. Finding joy. Living out love in every realm of your life.

You know that love isn't just something you give to others. Every day, you practice loving yourself. Forgiving yourself. You know you must so you can be whole. You know your son is watching. You want him to grow to love himself, too, so that—if it's God's will—he may one day love someone in a way that is patient and kind.

You are loved. And because you are, you can forgive. Your commitment to loving yourself as God loves you demands forgiveness and the boundaries that it brings. So you have released people from your life, including your abuser. Especially him. Neither he nor his devotees and defenders have any hold over you. Their critiques carry no water. Their words, if they have any, are for God. You don't need them. You know that God can sort all that out without you, and you are happy to let God do just that.

As you forgive those relatives who looked without seeing, who saw without watching you, you may choose to build a new relationship with them, one in which you're not held hostage to the secrets they wanted you to keep. While you can't reclaim lost time, you can claim a fresh start now. Maybe some of them will want this because you are standing before them, fully alive and able to speak. Maybe some won't. That's okay, too. Your healing isn't dependent upon their agreement, just as theirs isn't dependent upon you.

Let go and let God.

No one else holds power over your mind, body, or spirit. It's taken a while for you to arrive at the sure footing of this knowledge, but it's a good place to be. This is your moment! It's good to be you. God willing, you have more living and loving and growing to do. Go live in your truth and walk in your light. Embrace this next chapter in your journey with anticipation that God will plant new dreams in the fertile soil of your heart.

Love you times infinity,
Reshona

EPILOGUE

SCARS OF GOLD

RECENTLY, A FRIEND SUGGESTED I listen to a sermon that one of the preachers at her church gave for her church's observance of Denim Day, an internationally recognized part of Sexual Assault Awareness Month (April) that shows solidarity with survivors of sexual violence. I really didn't want to. I've heard too many folks say the wrong thing about sexual violence. I didn't need to hear someone talk out the side of their face from the pulpit.

My friend didn't push it...but she did share her sermon notes with me. Surprisingly, my long-winded friend had written down only three sentences:

Restoration doesn't necessarily mean that something will be the same. When we are restored, we may be made new and better, but not the same as we were before. Our cracks are filled with gold.

The last sentence made my eyes shiny with tears: *Our cracks are filled with gold.*

Yes.

I am scarred from the experiences I've shared and many more that I refuse to immortalize in the pages of this book.

I have been broken, and my wounds have spilled blood.

I look different. Maybe I even sound different than I did before.

Perhaps I would have been different than I am if these things had never happened to me.

But because I am a child of God, my wounds have healed in the most beautiful and unexpected ways. **I have scars of gold.**

ACKNOWLEDGMENTS

I could not have conquered this journey alone. I truly thank God for surrounding me with the right village. It's my honor to acknowledge a chosen few who stood by me when I needed it most.

To my son

This story is dedicated to you. Thank you for coming into my life; you saved me. You gave me a reason to live at a time when I felt hopeless. I no longer live in shame about my truth. I know you may one day face challenges because of my story, but always hold your head high and remember: Every wound made your mother a stronger, better woman.

To my dad

I wish you were here to see the woman I've become—to see me face my fears and bury my tears. In every moment of weakness, I found strength and admiration in you. Before you left this earth, you took accountability for things the world may never understand, and for that, I love you deeply.

To my beloved brother, Gregory Landfair Jr.

You carried so much at such a young age and made countless sacrifices for me. Thank you for always being brave and never leaving my side.

To my mom

I love you. I couldn't do life without you. You never gave up on me or walked away. Thank you for teaching me the true meaning of unconditional love and what it truly means to be a parent.

To Jonette Dixon

Words will never fully express the love and gratitude I have for you and our friendship. There was never a time I needed you and you weren't there. I couldn't write in a diary, but you held me down in private without judgment. Thank you, best.

To Christopher Brown

You kept your promise to my father, and you continue to protect me to this day. Thank you for being a trustworthy, reliable man of your word—and for always believing in me.

To Erica Simone Turnipseed

You were truly God-sent. No one else could have captured my emotions the way you did. You knew what my mind was thinking and how my heart felt. Writing with you was therapeutic, and I am truly grateful for you.

To Liz Nealon

Meeting you was life-changing for me. Thank you for steering me in the right direction and believing in me.

To Krishan Trotman and the Legacy Lit team

Thank you for seeing the power in my story. Because of you, I've been blessed with the opportunity to uplift other women and be a light through my journey.

AFTERWORD

AS DIFFICULT AS IT was for me to write this book, I know that I'm far from the only one to experience grooming and sexual abuse as a child and young woman. There are so many people—including some of you—who recognized aspects of their experience in mine. I'm so sorry that you were violated. I see you. I believe you.

If you don't get anything else from this book, please know this:

- you are not to blame for your abuse,
- you are not the worst thing that happened to you, and
- you can heal.

There are lots of people and organizations that can help you be safe and whole physically, mentally, emotionally, and spiritually. What I'm sharing here is just a small portion of those supports in the United States. Lots of cities and states have their own programs and services as well. Other countries also have resources; I included information on some of those, too.

- *If you're in immediate danger,* **CALL 911:** Be sure to enable location services on your cell phone. Some areas offer the feature of texting 911, but even if that's not available where you are, you can call and leave the line open so 911 can hear what's happening and send help to your location.
- *If you're considering self-harm,* **CALL 988:** The nationwide Suicide & Crisis Lifeline routes you to a crisis counselor who will talk to you and provide you with additional resources in your area. You can also text, chat, or receive deaf and hard-of-hearing services through the website: **988lifeline.org**.
- *If you are experiencing domestic violence,* **CALL 1-800-799-SAFE (7233):** The National Domestic Violence hotline can help you to safeguard yourself and your loved ones while you develop an exit plan.
- *Teachers, school administrators, social workers, and medical professionals can help:* If you go to school or college, or if you receive medical care from a nurse or doctor, plenty of people at schools and health clinics are mandated reporters. They can help you get the support you need and keep you safe.
- *Clergy members, after-school program directors, and other adults may be able to help:* Other adults in your community can help, including a parent/caregiver or relative, a parent of a close friend, a trusted member of the clergy at your place of worship, or a director or supervisor at an after-school program or activity you do.

In addition to that short list of emergency resources and trusted adults in your community, here are some organizations that can help you get whatever you need. I've included the organizations' websites and a paragraph from each site that explains what the organization does.

Black Women's Blueprint

https://restoreny.org/black-womens-blueprint/

"Black Women's Blueprint, which now lives inside Restore Forward, provides spaces and services designed by and for Black women and survivors to heal from trauma and violence."

Girls for Gender Equity

https://ggenyc.org/programs/

"Girls for Gender Equity (GGE) works intergenerationally to center the leadership of Black girls and gender-expansive young people of color in reshaping culture and policy through advocacy, youth-centered programming, and narrative shift to achieve gender and racial justice."

"me too." International

https://metoomvmt.org/

"'me too.' International is a survivor-led movement to end sexual violence through survivor and community healing programs, community organizing, narrative change, and resource building."

MCSR (formerly Men Can Stop Rape)

https://mcsr.org/ourvision

"Rooted in community, based in strength, and grounded in respect, MCSR prevents violence through transformational programs and services for youth and adults that promote healthy masculinity and empowered womanhood."

National Organization of Sisters of Color Ending Sexual Assault

https://sisterslead.org/

"The National Organization of Sisters of Color Ending Sexual Assault (SCESA) is an advocacy organization of Women of Color dedicated to working with our communities to create a just society in which all Women of Color are able to live healthy lives free of violence."

National Sexual Violence Resource Center

https://www.nsvrc.org/

"The National Sexual Violence Resource Center is the leading nonprofit in providing information and tools to prevent and respond to sexual violence. NSVRC translates research and trends into best practices that help individuals, communities, and service providers achieve real and lasting change. The center also works with the media to promote informed reporting."

National Tribal Clearinghouse on Sexual Assault (NTCSA)

https://www.miwsac.org/national-programs/clearinghouse/

"The NTCSA is a comprehensive resource hub that supports our Tribal communities with resources and education dedicated to improving the response to sexual assault by increasing access to culturally appropriate training and technical assistance with a focus on sovereignty, victim safety, and offender accountability."

Pathways to Safety International

https://pathwaystosafety.org/

"Pathways to Safety International educates Americans traveling and living abroad, offers tools to stay informed about gender-based violence, and empowers victims to survive and heal."

Prevent Together

https://preventtogether.org/

"Prevent Together—The National Coalition to Prevent Child Sexual Abuse and Exploitation is a unified effort to promote the healthy development of children and youth and end child sexual abuse and exploitation, providing concrete, actionable steps that individuals, advocates, organizations, and communities can take to better protect children."

RAINN

https://rainn.org/

"RAINN (Rape, Abuse, and Incest National Network), the nation's largest anti–sexual violence organization, created and operates the 24/7, confidential National Sexual Assault Hotline: 800-656-HOPE (4673). RAINN also carries out programs to prevent sexual violence, help survivors, help organizations improve their sexual assault prevention and response programs, and ensure that perpetrators are brought to justice."

The Swan Center for Advocacy & Research, Inc.

https://www.swancenteradvocacy.org/

"The Swan Center is a Georgia-based nationally serving 501(c)(3) that works to value the lived experiences and safety of Black folks. Through crisis intervention, community outreach, and innovative research, it builds capacity for activism, cultural change, and survivor resiliency."

Ujima: The National Center on Violence Against Women in the Black Community

https://ujimacommunity.org/

"Ujima's mission is to inspire and support the Black community in responding to and preventing domestic and community violence and sexual assault. With a focus on collective responsibility and shared prosperity, we leverage our resources, expertise, and networks to cultivate a world where Black women and girls thrive."

We, As Ourselves

https://weasourselves.org/

"We, As Ourselves is a collaboration, powered by the 'me too' Movement, National Women's Law Center, and TIME'S UP Foundation, to reshape the narrative around sexual violence and its impact on Black survivors."

NOTES

1 Robert S. Kelly, letter to author, undated [winter 2005–2006].

2 "'He has to stop,' Sparkle said when she caught her breath, 'There have been too many to count. They definitely had to be young. His whole MO, he stated this to me long ago, he likes them when they are ripe and young because he can mold them into what he wants them to be and control their minds and make them do what women 'should' do. That's what he thinks, you know, be a servant, be the 'yes.'" Jim DeRogatis, *Soulless: The Case Against R. Kelly* (Abrams, 2019), 119.

3 Jane Doe [Reshona Landfair], "Trial Testimony," United States of America v. Robert Sylvester Kelly, also known as "R. Kelly," Derrel McDavid, and Milton Brown, also known as "June Brown," Case No. 19 CR 567 (U.S. District Court for the Northern District of Illinois, Eastern Division, August 18, 2022), at 753–759.

4 Ibid., 787–790.

5 Jane Doe [Reshona Landfair], "Trial Testimony," United States of America v. Robert Sylvester Kelly, also known as "R. Kelly," Derrel McDavid, and Milton Brown, also known as "June Brown," Case No. 19 CR 567 (U.S. District Court for the Northern District of Illinois, Eastern Division, August 19, 2022), at 875–876.

6 Ibid., 889–890.

7 Ibid., 893–894.

8 Jane Doe [Reshona Landfair], "Victim Impact Statement," United States of America v. Robert Sylvester Kelly, also known as "R. Kelly," Derrel McDavid, and Milton Brown, also known as "June Brown," Case No. 19 CR 567 (U.S. District Court for the Northern District of Illinois, Eastern Division, February 23, 2023), at 19–24.

RAISING READERS

Books Build Bright Futures

Thank you for reading this book and for being a reader of books in general. We are so grateful to share being part of a community of readers with you, and we hope you will join us in passing our love of books on to the next generation of readers.

Did you know that reading for enjoyment is the single biggest predictor of a child's future happiness and success?

More than family circumstances, parents' educational background, or income, reading impacts a child's future academic performance, emotional well-being, communication skills, economic security, ambition, and happiness.

Studies show that kids reading for enjoyment in the US is in rapid decline:

- In 2012, 53% of 9-year-olds read almost every day. Just 10 years later, in 2022, the number had fallen to 39%.
- In 2012, 27% of 13-year-olds read for fun daily. By 2023, that number was just 14%.

Together, we can commit to **Raising Readers** and change this trend. How?

- Read to children in your life daily.
- Model reading as a fun activity.
- Reduce screen time.
- Start a family, school, or community book club.
- Visit bookstores and libraries regularly.
- Listen to audiobooks.
- Read the book before you see the movie.
- Encourage your child to read aloud to a pet or stuffed animal.
- Give books as gifts.
- Donate books to families and communities in need.

BOB1217

Books build bright futures, and **Raising Readers** is our shared responsibility.

For more information, visit **JoinRaisingReaders.com**

Sources: National Endowment for the Arts, National Assessment of Educational Progress, WorldBookDay.com, Nielsen BookData's 2023 "Understanding the Children's Book Consumer"